30 Reasons
Employees Hate
Their Managers

30 Reasons Employees Hate Their Managers

What *Your* People May Be Thinking and
What You Can Do About It

Bruce L. Katcher
with
Adam Snyder

AMACOM
American Management Association
New York • Atlanta • Brussels • Chicago • Mexico City • San Francisco
Shanghai • Tokyo • Toronto • Washington, D.C.

Special discounts on bulk quantities of AMACOM books are available to corporations, professional associations, and other organizations. For details, contact Special Sales Department, AMACOM, a division of American Management Association, 1601 Broadway, New York, NY 10019.
Tel: 212-903-8316. Fax: 212-903-8083.
E-mail: specialsls@amanet.org
Website: www.amacombooks.org/go/specialsales
To view all AMACOM titles go to: www.amacombooks.org

This publication is designed to provide accurate and authoritative information in regard to the subject matter covered. It is sold with the understanding that the publisher is not engaged in rendering legal, accounting, or other professional service. If legal advice or other expert assistance is required, the services of a competent professional person should be sought.

Library of Congress Cataloging-in-Publication Data

Katcher, Bruce Leslie
    30 reasons employees hate their managers : what your people may be thinking and what you can do about it / Bruce L. Katcher with Adam Snyder.
      p. cm.
    Includes bibliographical references and index.
    ISBN-10: 0-8144-0915-6
    ISBN-13: 978-0-8144-0915-2
    1. Supervision of employees.   2. Industrial relations.   3. Personnel management. 4. Interpersonal relations.   I. Snyder, Adam.   II. Title.   III. Title: Thirty reasons employees hate their managers.

HF5549.12.K38   2007
658.3'02—dc22   2006028980

Printing number

10 9 8 7 6 5 4

Dedicated to the memory of my father, Milton (Mickey) Katcher. His incredibly strong work ethic and Job-like perseverance in the face of adversity in his personal and work-life has been a continuing source of inspiration to me.

Contents

Foreword

I t is business's dirty little secret. Put simply, the work environment for today's employees, no matter the industry or location, has deteriorated badly in recent years. At the same time America's workers are being placed under tremendous pressure to produce more in less time and with fewer resources, the traditional benefits of full-time employment are being eroded.

To a great extent, the problem is an outgrowth of management's abdication of their longstanding responsibility to provide leadership. By the mid-1990s, we started to hear the phrase that "we're all self-employed," signifying that we no longer were all in this together, but rather it was every man and woman for themselves. This concept was strongly embraced by corporate leadership . . . much more than it was by their employees. The result was a significant shattering of the bond between management and employee.

Just as the "we're all self-employed" phase began to lose steam, industry was confronted with the economic downturn at the turn of the century. In response, managers put even more pressure on their employees to produce more—faster and at less cost. Already-strained relationships between management and employees intensified.

In a perfect world, or in a perfect economy, dissatisfied employees would find employment elsewhere. Competition for the best workers would improve conditions for everyone. In fact, however, in a negative environment, employees often lose their confidence. They don't feel comfortable leaving their nest no matter how bad the situation. As a result, their performance continues to spiral downward, becoming a financial drag to their place of employment.

Is there any hope then? Most definitely there is. In the first place, despite the overall rather bleak environment for most workers, there are some companies that have combined impressive financial results with a policy of fully engaging their employees. These companies understand that most employees want to be successful and want to play a key role in the growth of their place of employment. In return for this strong commitment, they ask to share in the rewards of their company's financial success, and to be understood. They want management to recognize and respect their concerns, and not to consider their needs as a lack of dedication to their work.

Managers within these stellar companies also understand that they have a lot at stake in their relationship with their employees. Most insightful corporate leaders recognize that one thing that separates a successful organization from one that is not is its ability to attract, develop, motivate, organize, and retain top-notch employees. Obviously these conditions do not exist in an environment in which employees hate their managers.

Bruce Katcher has put together a management tool kit that quite simply could transform a negative situation within the workplace to one of great promise. Employees should also take heed. There are a number of practical suggestions in the following pages that can open the door to constructive improvements in the management-employee relationship, leading to improved business results.

Bob Gatti
President, Gatti & Associates
Specializing in the Search and Placement of
Human Resource Professionals

Acknowledgments

I would first like to thank my clients for partnering with me to help make their organizations more productive and satisfying places to work. Together we strive to find the appropriate balance between business realities and treating employees humanely.

Thank you to my wife Trinka and my children Ben and Melanie, who have always been tremendously supportive of my work.

Thank you to my sister, Andrea Brudnicki, whose trying work history has provided me with an endless supply of examples of the mistakes made by management.

Thank you to my colleagues at the Society of Professional Consultants, who have given me strength, friendship, and intellectual support.

Finally, thank you to my brother-in-law and good friend, Adam Snyder, for helping me put my ideas into a coherent and readable form.

30 Reasons Employees Hate Their Managers

Introduction

Employees hate management. Hate is a strong word, but in this case it's appropriate. Employees hate management because they feel they're treated with disrespect. They don't trust what management tells them. They feel underpaid and that their income is being squeezed because they are forced to shoulder more and more of the cost of their retirement and health benefits. They also believe their jobs have a negative impact on their quality of life. Most feel powerless to do anything about these concerns, which only increases their frustration. They're fearful of losing their jobs and believe that even if they were to find new employment, they would only encounter the same problems.

How do I know all this? I know it because since 1993 my company has been studying how employees view their work and what organizations can do to improve the workplace. Clients use our services when they want to gain an objective, quantitative understanding of what their employees are thinking. Employees are often leery of telling management how they really feel. At Discovery Surveys, we serve as an objective conduit of these thoughts and feelings. During a typical employee survey program, I meet with senior management to learn about their business and gain an understanding of what they really need to know from their employees. I also have the opportunity to meet face-to-face with employees to learn what's really on their minds and what they want management to know. These different perspectives help shape my understanding of the climate of the organization.

The Discovery Surveys, Inc.'s Normative Database, which is the source of the statistics in this book, represents the views of more than

1

50,000 employees from sixty-five organizations. They are about evenly split between manufacturing and service organizations, and range in size from 150 to 5,000 employees. Most are U.S. companies, but many have employees elsewhere. Several are based overseas.

Worker unhappiness is a problem for employees, to be sure. It obviously affects their quality of life. But it's also a serious problem for an organization's bottom line. Although few employees will actually come out and tell management they're unhappy, many instead demonstrate passive-aggressive behaviors in ways that are harmful to the organization. It may take the form of keeping good suggestions to themselves or intentionally doing the least amount of work possible. Others may insidiously turn their coworkers against their organization, or feel no remorse in taking advantage of it in other ways. The point is that when employees refuse to fully commit to the goals of your organization, productivity declines, customer satisfaction suffers, and profits are almost always adversely affected.

Does management care? Are they listening to the cries of employees? In most cases the answer is "no," and that's self-defeating.

But it doesn't have to be this way. The purpose of this book is to help managers and human resource professionals understand why their employees are unhappy and what they can do to make their workplace a more friendly and productive environment. Managers pore over tons of data to manage their business. They read daily financial reports about sales, expenses, and assets. But in a competitive environment in which employee productivity is a crucial asset, a quantitative report on the psychological health of employees is an equally important tool.

Each of the five parts of this book addresses a specific issue that our research shows is of particular concern to employees. For example, Part I describes how employees complain that they are not given the freedom they need to perform their work and feel that they are treated like children. It then discusses how managers can treat employees more like adults.

In many organizations, managers don't respect the work of employees, and employees don't respect the decisions made by managers. Part II discusses how to break this vicious cycle.

Many employees also do not feel managers provide them with enough qualified staff, training, or direction to properly perform their work. They also believe their organization is operating inefficiently. Part III discusses how to provide employees with what they really need to do their work, and how to avoid excessive red tape, lack of communication between departments, and poorly run meetings.

Many employees feel unappreciated by their managers, and that they have little chance of receiving the pay increases and promotions they feel they deserve. Part IV discusses what managers can do to address these concerns.

And finally, Part V discusses how managers can help employees avoid feeling distant and uncommitted to their organization, viewing their work as "just a job," with no commitment to or from the organization.

Within these parameters, each of the thirty chapters describes a specific problem, and explains some of the psychological theories that provide insight into why employees feel like slaves, and why many employers feel like masters. Each chapter also outlines specific steps management can take to make the work environment a more productive and satisfying place for both employees and management.

Part I

Employees Are Treated Like Children

Forty-six percent of all employees believe management treats them with disrespect.

We feel like slaves.

I telephoned my sister one morning at her office. She was working in the credit and collections department of a small medical equipment rental firm. We had been speaking for less than a minute when she told me that she had better hang up. She had just received an e-mail message from her supervisor sarcastically asking her if she was on break. The next day she found out that her boss was actually reading her private e-mails and listening to her private telephone conversations. Needless to say, she was outraged. But what could she do? The company had a legal right to spy on her and she desperately needed the job. She felt like a slave.

Employment is a form of slavery. This is a provocative analogy and may be offensive to some, but it is key to understanding why employees are often unhappy.

Merriam Webster defines a slave as, "a person who has lost control of himself or herself and is dominated by something or someone else."[1] This is precisely what happens in the workplace. Many employees, shackled to their jobs with little freedom to control their day-to-day work or career, feel like slaves.

Employees are "dominated" because their employer controls *what* they do, *when* they do it, and *where* they do it. In return for pay and benefits, employees must conform to set work hours, dress codes, and work rules. They must dutifully follow management's orders and maintain good relationships with their supervisors and coworkers. Many have very little say in how they perform their work. In short, they are like slaves because their employer controls their time, their space, and their actions.

Like masters of slaves, management often doesn't listen to employee suggestions or value their opinions. Indeed, they often don't even communicate directly with their employees. They communicate instead through middle managers or supervisors. Like slaves, employees are subject to the whims of management. Promises made by management are often broken with little explanation or remorse. It is not uncommon for employees to experience layoffs, salary reductions, increases in what they must pay toward their benefits, and the loss of their hard-earned pension benefits. It is also not uncommon for the senior managers (the "masters") to at the same time take home large salaries for themselves.

The Problem for Employers

Employees who are treated like slaves begin to feel and act like slaves. They live in a state of perpetual anxiety about not pleasing management and losing their jobs. Our research shows that 43 percent of all employees feel insecure about their jobs. These anxious employees typically lose self-confidence and are not the best performers. They become reluctant to express their useful opinions or to develop innovative approaches to their work.

Technically, of course, unlike slaves, employees are voluntary workers and are legally free to leave whenever they please. In practice, however, for many this is not the case. They may feel trapped. They don't want to leave their work friends or the "security" of their jobs. They are intimidated by the prospect of finding other employment. They silently resent management for their predicament.

The Psychology of It All

In the summer of 1971, Stanford University social psychologist Philip Zimbardo and his colleagues conducted a simulation of prison life in order to investigate the psychological effects of becoming both a prisoner and a prison guard.[2] Twenty-four male college students who had answered a newspaper ad to earn $15 a day to participate in a two-week study were randomly assigned to be either guards or prisoners. A mock prison was set up on campus in the basement of the psychology department.

Guards were given minimal instructions except to keep order. They were free to make up their own rules. Almost immediately the guards attempted to exert their authority by demeaning and dehumanizing the prisoners. Prisoners were stripped naked for delousing and were given uniforms and numbers. Their heads were shaved and they were placed in ankle locks in their cells. The prisoners, while at first compliant, grew angry and eventually tried to exert their independence by attempting a rebellion. When the rebellion was squashed, the prisoners grew weary and very upset and the guards grew even more abusive. Although individuals were randomly assigned to be either prisoners or guards, they each began to exhibit all the stereotypical behaviors of their real counterparts. Zimbardo reported that, "In only a few days, our guards became sadistic and our prisoners became depressed and showed signs of extreme stress."

This study is one of many to show that the behaviors of individuals are, to a large extent, dictated by the roles they are asked to assume rather than anything about themselves such as their skills or personalities. This same phenomenon occurs in the workplace. Management and employees are placed in roles with certain responsibilities and duties. These roles influence and feed off each other. For example, when management treats employees autocratically and disrespectfully, employees act subservient and resentful. Likewise, when employees acquiesce to management's will and direction, management becomes even more assertive. No matter how it starts, the cycle of master and slave behaviors continues and is difficult to reverse.

The perpetual state of anxiety experienced by many employees is due to what psychologists call a loss of the "perception of control." Studies have shown that the *perceived* control over one's destiny has more of an influence on anxiety than does the *actual* control. Employees feel like slaves because they lose the belief that they have control of their work lives. They become compliant and reluctant to exert their independence because they believe they have no choices. This makes them unhappy and anxious.

According to professor David Gershaw of Arizona Western College, psychologists reported that post-traumatic anxiety in aircrews during World War II was highest among the bomber crews, less among bomber pilots, and least among fighter pilots. Ironically, fighter pilots had the highest casualty rate among the three groups, even though they had the most control of their environment. Thus it was the *perceived* control and not the *actual* control that determined their level of anxiety.[3]

Many of my colleagues are independent consultants expressly because they want control over their working lives. A great many of them left corporate positions to start home-based businesses. Most have told me that once they experienced the freedom and control that came with operating outside of the corporate environment, it became almost impossible for them to even consider going back to this anxiety-ridden life. They relish the freedom of deciding what work they are going to perform, and where and when they are going to do it.

➲ Solutions

Becoming a benevolent master is not enough. Unshackling employees requires breaking the cycle of management control and employee acquiescence by respecting employees and giving them more control. Here are a few suggestions for how to emancipate employees by breaking the cycle of the master-employee relationship:

1. Respect employee privacy.

Masters feel they have every right to invade the privacy of slaves. Management should never, under any conditions, spy on employees. Legal or not, reading personal e-mails and listening in on personal telephone calls is a terrible invasion of privacy. You must have a clear business rationale for monitoring communications of an employee and you must do so openly. If you don't trust your employees, document their performance issues and take appropriate actions. But don't treat them as if they are your possessions and assume you can infringe on their privacy whenever you like.

2. Treat employees as valued business partners.

Masters have a dim view of the capabilities of slaves. Management should go out of its way to respect the advice and counsel they receive from employees. Many times managers who hired me to help them better understand how employees feel about working for the organization have confided to me, "I have told senior management many times about the problems here, but if you, an outside consultant, tell them, they might believe it." It is common in organizations for senior management to not respect the middle managers they hired to advise them.

3. Be honest with employees.

Masters feel it is within their rights to lie to slaves. It is not within the rights of managers to lie to their employees.

A 500-employee research organization with a long history of growth and prosperity had run into some financial difficulties. The Board of Directors put a new management team in place, and shortly thereafter the new president implemented a 10-percent layoff. He then met with employees in small groups to explain why it was necessary and to promise there would be no further layoffs for the foreseeable future. The very next week four more employees were laid off. The president said it was a restructuring and not a layoff, but the employees didn't buy it. His credibility was crushed and the morale of the organization took a tailspin that will take many years, and perhaps a new president, to reverse.

Honesty is always the best policy when communicating to employees. Of course, there will be times when managers cannot share certain information, but lying is never justified.

4. Encourage employee independence.

Masters tell slaves that this is just the way it is, like it or not. Slaves remain silent for fear of losing their lives. Employees may not like what management tells them to do, but they don't complain or question out of fear of losing their jobs.

To break the perceived bonds of slavery, encourage employees to be proactive and assertive. Support rather than reject out of hand employee demands for better work tools, more information about the direction of the organization, and increased decision-making authority.

5. Provide more opportunities for employees to control their work hours.

Slaves have no control of their work hours. Many employees don't either.

I have consistently found that many of the happiest employees are those who work part-time. Why is this? They typically make less money, receive few if any benefits, are less involved in organizational decision-making, and are less connected to the people in the office. They are happier because they perceive more control over their own time. Even though they abide by the normal working hours on the days they are scheduled to work, they do not feel like slaves to the clock. Instead, they feel they have control over when they work. They therefore feel more independent (and less slave-like) than those who work full-time.

Some jobs, of course, require someone to be at their desk full-time. A customer service representative has to be near the telephone during all the organization's normal working hours. However, ask yourself if it would be more beneficial for you to have one employee at the station half the week and another, equally competent person at that station for the other half. Offer employees who convert to part-time work the opportunity to maintain their health benefits.

If you hire more part-time workers, you will have a happier and more productive workforce. Besides, when given the opportunity, many salaried employees can complete a full weeks' worth of work in less than a week. Let them do it. After all, are you paying for the work to be completed, or for hours logged on the time clock?

6. Provide more opportunities for employees to control their work space.

Slaves, like employees, have little say about where they work. Many organizations have discovered that employees can be just as effective, if not more so, working from their homes rather than reporting to the office. Employees who report to the office waste valuable time and energy commuting and chatting by the coffee pot. Most business today is transacted by telephone and e-mail anyway. Employees can do this just as easily from their homes.

Employees who work primarily out of their homes are more satisfied with their work life than those who work in an office. Although these home-working employees are less involved in organizational decision making and less connected to their colleagues in the office, they feel they have more control. They don't have to be sitting at their desks or beside the phone projecting a compliant image to their boss. They are in *control* of their "space."

7. Support professional development.

Masters do not allow their slaves to escape, but employers should. Support employees in their efforts to develop professionally and perhaps leave the organization for a better opportunity. If employees believe their current job is just one temporary stop in their chosen career, they will feel more in control of their work life. Managers should actually encourage their employees to keep an eye out for their next job by always maintaining an up-to-date resume, attending professional networking groups, maintaining relationships with former coworkers, and keeping in touch with search firms. It's also a good idea to provide career counseling and professional development opportunities.

Such support for employees is not merely altruistic. It will further the goals of the organization by keeping a cadre of highly motivated, accomplished, and upwardly mobile employees who refuse to become complacent slaves. It will also be attractive to potential new employees to know that the organization supports employee growth and development.

Conclusion

Organizations do not own employees like masters own slaves. The vicious cycle—management treating employees disrespectfully and employees acquiescing, feeling unhappy, resentful, and powerless—can be stopped. It is in the self-interest of employers to provide their employees with as much freedom as possible and to support their desire for more control of how, when, and where they perform their work.

Notes

1. *Merriam-Webster Online Dictionary*: m-w.com.

2. P. G. Zimbardo and G. White, Stanford Prison Experiment Slide-Tape Show (Stanford University, 1972): prisonexp.org.

3. David Gershaw, Jiskha Homework Help: jiskha.com/social_stud ies/psychology/.

❷

Forty percent of employees say they don't have the decision-making authority they need to do their jobs well, and 63 percent believe that decisions in their company are usually not made at the appropriate level.

I know how to do my job.
Why can't they just let me do it?

Rick is a competent and experienced human resources professional who has been with the organization many years. His boss is a micromanager. She is very controlling, constantly second-guesses his decisions, and wants the final say on everything. Rick feels like a prisoner whose voice goes unheard by the senior executives of his company because his boss allows him only very minimal contact with them.

Needless to say, coming to work each day is very difficult for Rick. He hates his boss. His creativity and enthusiasm for his work are low and he feels that he is never going to be able to realize his full potential. He wears his emotions on his sleeve and walks through the organization moping with a sour look on his face. His job performance has been in a downward spiral for several years. He has become argumentative and an emotional drain on his colleagues. He knows this, but feels powerless to do anything about it. He has discussed the issue many times with his boss and even his boss's boss, but to no avail. He feels trapped. He has been looking for another job, but hasn't been able to find a comparable position elsewhere.

Rick wishes his boss would just leave him alone and let him make

decisions as he sees fit. He is perfectly willing to suffer the consequences if those decisions prove to be unwise.

The Problem for Employers

A culture in which employees are micromanaged and not given
decision-making authority leads to an unhappy, unproductive, paralyzed workforce that lacks self-motivation and is unable to take prudent business risks or develop innovative ideas.

Employees are selected to work in organizations because they possess certain skills and knowledge. It is wasteful if your organization
does not allow them to use their skills and knowledge to their full
potential. If the activities of individuals are artificially constrained, the
overall performance of the organization will suffer. It is management's responsibility to provide a supportive environment in which
employees are empowered to contribute to their fullest.

The Psychology of It All

There are a number of reasons why organizations fail to provide employees with the decision-making authority they need.

1. *Top-Down Mirroring.* The CEO or president micromanages direct staff. The staff then unconsciously adopts the same management
style with *their* direct reports. According to my dissertation adviser,
Kenwyn Smith, the practice can spread or mirror itself throughout the
organization and becomes an immutable part of the culture.[1]

2. *Too Many Chiefs, Not Enough Indians.* Some organizations have
an overabundance of middle managers. To justify their existence,
these managers mistakenly feel they need to make all the decisions for
their employees.

3. *Externally-Imposed Paranoia.* Highly regulated organizations,
such as food manufacturers, pharmaceutical companies, and nuclear
power generation plants, frequently suffer from micromanagement.

Employees are given very little latitude to deviate from standard operating procedures. The unfortunate result is that some of these employees learn to avoid thinking for themselves even when such thinking is critically important, such as during emergencies.

4. *Fear.* In today's difficult economy managers live in perpetual fear that their department better produce or else. This fear drives them to micromanage rather than trust their employees to make the appropriate decisions.

5. *Inability to Surrender Control.* You've heard the expression, "If you want anything done right, you've got to do it yourself." Many parents have a difficult time asking their children to clean their rooms, do the laundry, or even take out the garbage. Instead, they take the easy way out and just do it themselves. Many managers act the same way.

6. *Inability to Delegate.* Many managers are willing to delegate, but don't know how. Delegation requires the ability to break up large tasks into smaller chunks, establish priorities, create timetables, and decide which of those pieces you need to perform yourself and which can be just as easily done by one of your direct reports. You will need to learn to monitor rather than micromanage the activities of your subordinates.

7. *Lack of Direction.* Managers often receive little guidance from *their* bosses about the importance of delegating. They need to be told to work on high value activities and not to waste their time doing work that can be done by others.

8. *Poor Hiring Decisions.* Many organizations do not make it a priority to select employees who are capable of thinking on their own. The organization is then compelled to micromanage them.

➲ Solutions

1. Make certain the senior executives delegate.
If senior managers don't delegate, it is unlikely that their direct reports will either. Senior managers need to set the appropriate example. Others will then likely follow suit.

2. Provide delegation training for managers.
Delegating, letting go, and trusting employees are all skills that can be taught. There are many training programs, books, and tapes that teach managers how to delegate. Require managers to read some of them or attend a few programs.

3. Share best practices.
Good role models can be very effective. Ask those managers who are doing a good job of delegating to share their "best practices" with other managers in the organization.

4. Ask managers to put themselves in their employees' shoes.
It is very easy for managers to lose perspective about what decisions their employees really need to make. Ask yourself what decisions you would make if you were performing that particular job.

5. Rate supervisors on how well they delegate.
Some companies track how well supervisors delegate. Each year employees are asked the extent to which they agree with the following statement, "I have the decision-making authority I need to do my job well." Those supervisors whose employees do not feel empowered are required to develop action plans for how they can deliver more decision-making authority to their employees. Some are also required to attend training sessions on the topic.

6. Ask employees what decision-making authority they really need.
Use focus groups and individual interviews to learn from employees what decision-making authority they feel they need to do their

jobs well. Then communicate this information to their supervisors. Better yet, require supervisors to meet with employees individually to discuss this issue.

7. Encourage employees to push back.

Just as teenagers need to scratch and claw to earn independence from their parents, employees need to push back on bosses. They need to make it clear what decision-making authority they need and reassure their bosses that they will use their authority properly. It is your responsibility to make certain the people who work for you push back to gain more control of their work.

8. Train employees how to exercise more decision-making authority.

Some employees will jump at the opportunity to make more decisions. However, many others will need to be coaxed and encouraged. They may have become complacent due to the micromanaging of their boss. Training will be needed to change attitudes and help them feel more comfortable taking over the reins.

Conclusion

Employees are not happy when they aren't free to make their own decisions. They hate management for not trusting them and not respecting their abilities. Managers should be taught and encouraged to delegate so that employees have the decision-making authority they need for a healthy organization. Employees should communicate what authority they really need and push back.

Note

1. K. K. Smith, "A Critical Paradox for Community Psychologists: The Phenomenon of Mirroring," delivered at the Australian Psychological Society Conference, Melbourne, Victoria, 1975.

3

Fifty-two percent of employees do not feel free to voice their opinions openly.

I am afraid to speak up.

During a pep talk to the troops, a brave U.S. soldier serving in Iraq dared to ask Secretary of Defense Donald Rumsfeld a challenging question. He asked why U.S. soldiers needed to scavenge through landfills to find armor to protect their vehicles. Speaking up in this way was shocking and received a great deal of international press attention. Soldiers are usually too intimidated to challenge their leaders.

The same holds true in many organizations. According to our Discovery Surveys Normative Database, only 48 percent of working employees feel free to voice their opinions. They feel it is safer to just keep their mouths shut. This is one more reason employees hate their managers.

At a local hospital I interviewed an X-ray technician, the senior person on the day shift who was held in high esteem by management. He told me that he and his manager repeatedly did not see eye to eye on certain work-related issues. He said that time after time the manager didn't even open himself up to the idea that he might have a good suggestion. From that point forward, he made up his mind he wouldn't speak up at all in his department. "If I have a suggestion," he told me, "I just keep it to myself. It's just a job for me now. I put in my eight hours, pick up my paycheck, and then enjoy my time at home." Management had lost the insights of a valuable employee.

This problem, pervasive in many organizations, also affects supervisory employees. I met one day with a group of forty middle level managers in a financial services company to discuss the results of their employee opinion survey. After sharing with them the survey finding that employees did not feel free to openly express their views, I asked the group, "Why do you think employees are too afraid to speak up?" There was no reply.

The Problem for Employers

It's a sad commentary that more than half of all employees are too scared to openly express their views at work. A lack of openness has negative consequences for both employers and employees. When employee don't feel free to speak up:

- Good ideas don't surface.
- Important problems go undetected.
- Vital information is not shared with others in the organization who need to know.
- Groups make faulty decisions because individuals are afraid to disagree.
- Valuable time is wasted at unproductive meetings.
- Relationships between managers and employees deteriorate.
- Motivation declines because employees view their work as no longer worth their full commitment.

The Psychology of It All

Employees don't speak up for a variety of reasons, including:

- *Weak Communication Skills.* Many employees do not possess the verbal skills to accurately express their views. They feel it is safer to keep their mouth shut than to speak in a way that might reflect badly upon them.

•   *Poor Emotional Intelligence.* The ability to express one's feelings in a tactful and appropriate manner in the work setting is beyond the skills of many employees.

•   *Fear of Retribution.* Many organizations foster a climate of "shooting the messenger" when bad news is expressed by an employee. Ever notice the deafening silence when a senior manager completes a presentation and asks a group of employees if there are any questions? One common reason this occurs is that in the past employees have witnessed others being ignored, belittled, or embarrassed when they spoke up.

•   *Job Insecurity.* In today's layoff-happy environment, employees feel it is best to "keep their mouths shut" whenever possible.

•   *Lack of Management Responsiveness.* When they voiced their opinions in the past, no one listened, so why should they risk doing so again?

•   *Uncaring Organizational Climate.* Many feel like a mere cog in a big, unfeeling machine, with very little chance of being heard.

➲ Solutions

1. Foster a spirit of openness.
Managers must consciously try to ask for opinions and then listen carefully. Listen more than you speak. Doing so will increase the probability that your direct reports will be open to new ideas. Also, continually thank employees for their suggestions. When appropriate, tell employees that their suggestions were heard and appreciated.

2. Catch people in the act and use positive reinforcement.
When employees make comments, suggestions, or criticisms, go out of your way to acknowledge the remarks. Sincerely thank

them, being careful not to be patronizing. This will not only increase the probability that they will speak up again, it will also promote a spirit of openness that will spread to others.

3. Improve your listening skills.

Listening is a critically important management skill that can help improve employees' willingness to speak up. Some of the key principles are:

- *Use unconditional positive regard.* Don't automatically discount suggestions from your employees. Try not to rush to judgment. View every employee with a positive outlook.

- *Dummy up.* Use the technique made famous by the actor Peter Falk in the role of the seemingly bumbling, but actually cagy detective, Lieutenant Columbo. If you don't understand or need more clarification, continually ask questions and tell employees you "don't understand" or "are confused."

- *Avoid threatening questions.* For example, questions like "Who told you to do it that way?" and "Who is responsible?" will restrict the type of responses you receive.

- *Be an active listener.* Be psychologically engaged when listening to employees. Techniques like maintaining eye contact, nodding your head at the appropriate times, and saying things like "I see" and "uh-huh" in response to their words can go a long way toward assuring employees that you are listening and value what they have to say.

- *Ask open-ended questions.* Questions like "How do you feel about this?" or "Could you please tell me more about that?" will elicit more than one-word answers.

- *Use restatements.* Simply repeating or paraphrasing what an employee has just said will typically encourage the person to continue speaking.

4. **Get in the habit of making self-disclosures.**
It can be contagious when senior managers display openness themselves. For example, a CEO could stand up in front of employees and say something like, "As you know, we recently made a decision to acquire another company but I had many doubts, such as. . . . What are your doubts?"

Conclusion

The fact that less than half of all employees feel free to voice their opinions in their organizations has a negative consequence for both employees and their organizations. When employees are reluctant to contribute their ideas or to question management, organizations cannot realize their full potential. Fostering a spirit of openness and improving your own listening skills will take a consistent effort by senior managers and supervisors, but the benefits to the organization will be substantial.

Forty-three percent of employees say their good work goes unrecognized.

Nobody appreciates my hard work.

M any of the employees at a small rural hospital in New England have more than twenty-five years of service. While most employees enjoy their work and the collegiality they have with their fellow employees, many of the nurses complain that the hospital does not adequately recognize their many years of service. They believe they shouldn't have to work weekends, should receive more vacation time, and should be paid significantly more than newly hired nurses.

At another organization, a small, family-owned manufacturing company, long-service employees are also concerned about their lack of recognition. As the organization has grown, employees who have been on the job for more than thirty years have begun to feel more like just paid help rather than part of the family. They wish their contributions would be better recognized by the owners and by their supervisors.

The Problem for Employers

Many employees are unhappy because they believe management does not respect their good work. They crave encouragement and positive feedback but feel their supervisors fail to praise them when they:

- Make good decisions.
- Take prudent business risks.
- Make important contributions during meetings.
- Come up with innovative ideas.

One of the signs of a healthy organization is a climate of positive reinforcement and recognition. Supervisors in these organizations can be frequently heard saying to their employees:

- "Good point."
- "I'm glad you brought that up."
- "I really appreciate that."
- "Good job."
- "Well done."
- "Thank you."

Here are six reasons why many managers fail to provide recognition to employees:

1. They take their employees for granted.

2. They view employees as expenses rather than investments and vital assets.

3. They don't realize how important praise and recognition really are to employees.

4. They lack an appropriate level of emotional intelligence. For them, thanking employees is awkward and just not part of their normal repertoire of interpersonal behavior.

5. They don't know how to tactfully thank or recognize employees in a way that will be perceived as genuine rather than patronizing.

6. They have never received recognition from their own supervisors.

The Psychology of It All

One of the most well-documented principles of psychology is that positive reinforcement increases the probability that a behavior will reoccur in the future.[1] Likewise, without positive feedback, desirable employee behaviors may not occur again. Worse, employees will become unhappy, unmotivated, and unproductive.

It is also well documented that positive reinforcement is much more effective than punishment for shaping behavior. Annual bonuses often do not have the desired reinforcing effect because employees often view these bonuses as entitlements, not as personal recognition for their good work. Sincere, heartfelt praise clearly articulated and provided at the right time is a much more powerful motivating force. Nevertheless, few supervisors take advantage of these principles when managing their employees. It is much more common for them to criticize, scold, berate, belittle, or ignore them.

➲ Solutions

1. **Use individual-based recognition instead of group recognition.**
Every year most employers provide group recognition to their employees in the form of lavish holiday parties, gift turkeys, or cash bonuses. Everyone receives the politically correct equal amount of recognition for loyalty and good performance. But as well intentioned as this might be, individuals often perceive this type of recognition as meaningless. What they want instead is personal recognition for their own individual contributions.

2. Accompany individual bonuses with an appropriate personal message.

Organizations that merely mail bonus checks to their employees are missing out on an excellent opportunity to sincerely communicate their appreciation. The check should be accompanied by a personal visit from a supervisor or senior manager in which personal thanks is provided. If this is not possible, at a minimum attach a personal note of thanks to the bonus check, along with specific details about their performance.

3. Provide immediate rather than after-the-fact recognition.

Research has shown that positive reinforcement is most effective when it immediately follows the desired behavior.[2] Although it is customary to provide employees with recognition at certain times of the year—such as during the annual performance review, at the end of the year, or at an employee's anniversary date—it is better to catch people in the act of doing good things and provide them with on-the-spot recognition. That makes it much clearer to the employee exactly why she is being lauded.

4. Train supervisors how to provide positive feedback.

Many supervisors would benefit greatly from learning the simple principles of positive feedback. For example, in addition to providing the feedback as soon as possible after the behavior, positive feedback should be of the proper magnitude to match the behavior. Public acknowledgement after an employee makes a good point would be more appropriate than providing a spot cash bonus, for example.

Behaviorists have also demonstrated that variable reinforcement is more effective than continuous reinforcement. For example, praising employees periodically on an irregular basis is more effective than praising them every time they do something well.

5. Make positive feedback part of the performance review process.
It has become a truism that "what gets measured gets done." Evaluate supervisors on how well they provide positive feedback to their staff. Make this part of their annual performance review.

6. Provide feedback about feedback.
One way to increase the amount of positive reinforcement that occurs in an organization is to reinforce the reinforcer. In other words, senior management should periodically reinforce supervisors when they provide positive feedback to their direct reports.

7. Senior management must serve as role models.
Positive reinforcement needs to start at the top. Senior management can set the tone by appropriately praising and recognizing their direct reports. Doing so on a consistent basis will eventually spread the process throughout the organization.

Conclusion

Employees are unhappy that they are not receiving the appropriate recognition for their work. They hate that management doesn't fully appreciate them. Many supervisors fail to understand that just a little positive feedback can be a very powerful management tool for increasing productivity. The dividends to the organization can be sizeable.

Notes

1. W. F. Whyte, "Skinnerian Theory in Organizations," *Psychology Today*, April 1972, pp. 67–68.

2. B. M. Bass and J. A. Vaughan, *Training in Industry: The Management of Learning* (Belmont, Calif.: Wadsworth, 1966).

❺

Fifty-three percent of all employees believe their organization is applying personnel policies and procedures unfairly.

There are different rules for different people.

I was consulting to a large New England-based insurance company to help them improve the morale and productivity of their workforce. During a series of focus groups employees in the customer service department told me they were very upset that they had been required to come to work in the snow and were not allowed to be late. It had been a very snowy winter and commuting to work had been a major challenge. They said that those in other departments were allowed to arrive later and even to work from home. They didn't believe this was fair.

In another example, a small public relations firm in Boston employs many bright, young employees straight out of college. They are constantly working under deadlines to complete press releases and other client projects. Many complained that they had to work well into the night, while some of the older workers were allowed to leave promptly at 5:00 P.M. every day to pick up their children at day-care centers. They didn't think it was fair that they had to work late just because they didn't have children. "We have personal lives too," they said.

Employees come to the workplace with the assumption that all employees will be treated equally. They resent the fact that certain people or groups receive what they perceive to be preferential treatment. Typical complaints include:

- Smokers get to take smoking breaks but nonsmokers don't.

- Some departments can choose to take vacation whenever they want, while others are restricted to specific weeks.

- Only in some departments can employees arrive to work late, leave early, and come and go as they please.

- Some employees don't pull their own weight here, but we all get the same pay.

- The salespeople get to take long lunches, but we have to be back at our desks promptly at 1:00 P.M.

- Management treats the doctors here like gods, but we—who do most of the work—are treated like second-class citizens.

- The good workers like me end up doing the most work because management knows I will get it done and do it well.

The Problem for Employers

When employees feel that personnel policies and procedures are not administered fairly they lose respect for management, build up resentment toward their fellow coworkers, and lose motivation to do their work.

Employees often confuse unequal treatment with a lack of fairness. They believe that all employees should be treated exactly the same regardless of their position, job responsibilities, or personal needs. But these complaints expose a common fallacy. Employees should always be treated fairly, of course. There should be no personnel decisions made on the basis of gender, age, national background, race, religion, sexual orientation, or disability. But that doesn't mean every employee should be treated exactly the same.

It is perfectly appropriate, for example, for superior performers to receive special benefits, increased pay, and more flexibility. It also makes sense for there to be different work rules for workers with different job responsibilities. Some jobs require precise start and stop times whereas others do not. Receptionists, for example, need to be in the front lobby during normal working hours, while sales personnel often must attend networking meetings during the evenings and weekends.

Do you have the same rules for your seven-year-old daughter and your seventeen-year-old son? Of course not. They are different, have different needs, different responsibilities, and different capabilities. They are treated fairly but not equally.

The Psychology of It All

It is important to employees that they feel respected for their hard work and good job performance. When they see others receiving special benefits and privileges, the unequal treatment makes them bitter and unhappy.

According to the "Equity Theory," developed by John Stacey Adams, employees seek balance with others in the organization between what they put into their job (e.g., effort, ability, commitment, and time) and what they get out of it (e.g., pay, recognition, advancement opportunities, and enjoyment).[1] Employees become frustrated when they feel that their ratio of inputs to outcomes is larger than the ratio of others. For example, if an employee feels she is performing very well on the job (i.e., high input) and is receiving the same pay (i.e., outcome) as someone with lower input (i.e., poor performance), she will become frustrated. Similarly, if an employee feels that management is providing more favor to others, the ratios will be unequal and he will become frustrated.

Equity theory further predicts that this frustration will lead people to try to reduce the inequity in one of five ways:

1. *Reduce one's own inputs.* Employees may reduce their own input by lowering the quality of their job performance.

2. *Increase one's own outcomes.* If the organization were to provide the employee with more pay, this would help to reduce the inequity. This, however, is not within the control of the frustrated individual. Another possibility is for the employee to change his perception of his own pay. For example, he could think about how he is paid more than his friends working in other organizations.

3. *Increase other people's inputs.* The frustrated employee could change his perception of the inputs of the poor performers. For example, he could tell himself, "Although my coworker isn't performing as well, she has worked very hard over the years and deserves to coast a little now." Or he could think, "There are many other intangibles that my coworker brings to the table, such as strong loyalty to the organization, serving on committees, or helping others do their job well."

4. *Reduce other people's outcomes.* The frustrated employee could try his best to reduce the pay of the coworker or even get that person fired by complaining about the situation to other employees, the supervisor, and senior management.

5. *Leave the field.* If none of the above solutions reduce the employee's frustration, he may decide to leave the situation.

➲ Solutions

1. Promote flexibility rather than rigid rules.

Many organizations make the mistake of becoming overly rule oriented. They produce personnel and procedure manuals as thick as telephone books and expect this will help ensure fairness. But rules are always subject to interpretation, and thick rulebooks can actually make it more rather than less difficult for supervisors. I have found that organizations that simply entrust supervisors to follow broad ethical guidelines to make day-to-day decisions about policies receive the fewest number of complaints about fairness.

Employees want to be treated as unique, mature individuals. They want to know that special exceptions will be made to accommodate their particular circumstances.

2. Communicate a philosophy of flexibility.

Make it clear to employees that everyone will be treated fairly, but not exactly the same. Communicate that you reserve the right to treat employees as individuals and to make exceptions to the rules.

3. Avoid the union mentality.

Unions work hard to negotiate contracts that contain detailed rules about how much workers must be paid. Their goal is to take pay decisions out of the hands of management. Most contracts stipulate that pay will be based on tenure, not job performance. However, I have found that in most unionized environments, union workers are very concerned because the most senior employees seem to work the least and earn the most. Ironically, this is what is specified in the union contract they pay their union to negotiate for them. You may be pleasantly surprised at the reaction of union representatives if you broached the subject of introducing pay for performance in addition to pay for years of service.

Conclusion

Employees hate management for what they perceive as a lack of fairness, but this is because they confuse fairness with unequal treatment. All employees should be treated fairly but not exactly the same. Carefully explain to your employees that organizations are meritocracies, not socialistic states. They should know that good performers will be treated differently from poor performers, that those with higher levels of responsibility will be treated differently from those with less responsibility, and that those who have special needs will be treated differently from those who do not. No apologies are necessary.

Note

1. J. S. Adams, "Toward an Understanding of Inequity," *Journal of Abnormal Psychology* 67 (1963): 422–436.

Part II

Employees Aren't Respected

*Sixty-six percent of all employees say management doesn't listen to them,
and 67 percent say management fails to act on employee suggestions.*

Management doesn't listen to us.

One day a concerned husband visited his doctor. He said, "Doc, I'm really worried. My wife appears to be going deaf. She never hears me and I don't know what to do." "Here is what I want you to do," said the doctor. "Go home and stand about fifteen feet away from her and say something. If she doesn't hear you, walk about five feet closer and try again. Keep doing this until she hears you. This will help us determine the severity of her hearing loss."

The man went home and peered into the entrance to the kitchen. He saw his wife chopping vegetables near the sink. He called out to her, "Honey, what's for dinner?" There was no reply. He then took three large steps closer and repeated, "Honey, what's for dinner?" Again, there was no reply. Now he started to get really worried. He walked up right behind her and said a third time, "Honey, what's for dinner?" She turned to him and said angrily, "For the third time, we're having stir-fried vegetables."

The problem was not that she couldn't hear. It was that *he* wasn't hearing her. This is a common problem in organizations. Management often complains that employees aren't listening, but it's really management who isn't listening to employees.

Several years ago, I was consulting to a large East Coast media company. My job was to survey employees in a printing company it had recently purchased. The results were very negative. Employees were especially dissatisfied with the still-in-charge former owner and his second-in-command son.

In a series of feedback sessions I shared the survey results with groups of forty to fifty employees at a time. The son sat in on the sessions. His job was to talk to employees after my presentation to tell them how the company planned to respond to their concerns.

One of the major findings was that employees felt that senior management did not listen to their suggestions. The son got up and announced, "If any of you at any time have any suggestions or anything you would like to say to me or my father, you can just *STICK IT IN THE BOX.*"

He then pointed to the locked unused suggestion box hanging on the wall. What message do you think that sent to employees? He was clearly saying, "We're really not interested in what you have to say." No wonder when he asked if there were any comments or questions, no one raised their hand.

The Problem for Employers

Employees are not happy when they know management isn't listening to them. Their motivation and commitment to the goals of the organization are sure to deteriorate if they feel management doesn't care about what they have to say.

Open communication of ideas and suggestions from employees to senior management is critical to the healthy functioning of any organization. Senior management needs to know what is happening in the trenches, how customers feel about the organization's products and services, how productivity and quality can be improved, and how costs can be reduced. One of the major lessons of the total quality improvement movement has been that employees who actually perform the work usually have very good suggestions for improvements. Ignoring their ideas is a sure prescription for inefficiency and reduced profitability.

How can employees trust the judgment of senior management when their good suggestions are ignored? Without this trust, their motivation and commitment to the organization declines. Ignoring their suggestions is a slap in the face. In time, employees reciprocate by showing a lack of respect to management and the goals of the organization.

I have often heard employees say, "I know they are throwing money down the drain, but there's no way I would tell management how to improve things. They would only ignore me." Organizations with this type of climate are destined to fail.

The Psychology of It All

Employees sometimes wonder how all those close-minded SOBs ended up in the boardroom. Is there some character or personality trait common to senior managers that make them ignore rank and file employees? There are at least four reasons why senior managers ignore employee input.

1. Relationships Among Groups Within an Organizational Hierarchy

The first reason why employees ignore employee input can be explained by something Kenwyn Smith describes as "the intergroup perspective." In any hierarchical system, the uppers (i.e., those in senior management) see the world differently from those in the middle of the organization (i.e., mid-level managers and supervisors), who in turn see things differently from those at the bottom (i.e., hourly workers). External factors such as the demand for the organization's products and services and the attitudes of stockholders shape the perspective of the uppers. By the necessities of their job, uppers typically spend very little time interacting with the lowers. They rely on the middles to manage the work of the lowers and to tell them what the lowers are saying. Uppers are thus often out of touch with the perspective of the lowers.[1]

When we don't interact with people who have perspectives different from our own, we typically don't trust them. Senior managers,
therefore, distrust the abilities and knowledge of the lowers. They
think that since the lowers see the world differently, they "just don't
get it." Likewise, lowers frequently say, "Management just doesn't
have a clue about what's really happening in this organization."

If you were to promote a lower-level manager to a senior management position, that person would soon develop the same disrespect of
the views of lowers. It's the position in the hierarchy, not the personality that plays a large role in shaping the trust senior managers have
for employees. Remember how the Zimbardo prison study demonstrated that behaviors are determined, in part, by roles.

2. The Role of Self-Fulfilling Prophesies

In 1968, psychologist Robert Rosenthal conducted an experiment with
a third-grade class in California. He gave the students an IQ test and
told the teachers that the test had identified students who were "late
bloomers" who would eventually show a spurt in their IQ. In reality,
Rosenthal randomly selected the 20 percent of the pupils he told
teachers were the late bloomers.[2]

After one year the students were given the IQ test again. Lo and
behold, those who had been falsely labeled as late bloomers actually
earned significantly higher IQ scores than the other students. Rosenthal's conclusion was that the teachers had both consciously and
unconsciously treated the late bloomers differently, which created a
self-fulfilling prophecy.

The same thing happens in reverse in the workplace. Managers
who distrust the ability and knowledge of employees communicate
this feeling to them—sometimes subtly, other times actively. When
their input and counsel aren't taken seriously, employees feel that
their opinions don't count and don't share them. Since managers consequently receive little good advice from them, their unwillingness to
seriously consider employee input grows.

3. The Faulty Assumption of Finite Power

A third reason why management doesn't listen to employees has to do with their view of power. Managers often mistakenly believe that there is a finite amount of power in an organization, and that it is their job to amass as much of it as possible. They also believe that knowledge and authority are the elements of power. As a result, they do not listen to employees because that would be surrendering their own power.

Nothing could be further from the truth. The more management listens to the perspectives of employees, the more powerful the entire organization and each member of the organization will be.

4. The Telephone Game

The final reason management doesn't listen to employees is that communications often become distorted. This is similar to the game of telephone we all played when we were children. The first person whispers a message to the second, who then whispers it to a third. At the end of the line, the message bears little resemblance to its original form or meaning.

In organizations, the "middles," such as supervisors and department heads, are sandwiched between senior management and the majority of the workers. Part of their job is to pass information back and forth between the two other groups. Paradoxically, they are the ones who often hinder this flow of communication.

➲ Solutions

1. Circumvent the hierarchy.

It is very easy for good suggestions to get lost in the hierarchy. Employees become frustrated when their supervisors (i.e., the middles) do not pass along their suggestions to senior management. Senior management should avoid the bureaucracy by conducting face-to-face meetings with employees. Meetings such as "bagels-with-the-president" and "brown-bag-lunches with the

CEO" can offer rich opportunities for senior mangers to discover useful ideas directly from employees.

2. Get rid of the "suggestion box."
There is no better way to stifle openness than to tell employees to use a suggestion box rather than to voice their views openly. Employees should be given the opportunity to voice their suggestions in person to senior management.

3. Set realistic expectations.
Employees are usually disappointed when their suggestions are not used, but in some cases they are off base or unrealistic. Management needs to make it clear that not every suggestion can be implemented, but that all suggestions are welcome. Employees with good suggestions will be satisfied that only the good suggestions are used.

4. Proactively promote the proliferation of suggestions.
Management should make it clear to employees that providing suggestions is an expected part of everyone's job.

5. Close the loop.
It is important for management to communicate to employees when their suggestions are being implemented. Public recognition or cash awards for good suggestions can be their own self-fulfilling prophecy. Such recognition, combined with the overall sense that employee suggestions are not being ignored, will increase the probability employees will continue to make useful suggestions.

Conclusion

Management often doesn't listen to employees and employees are not happy about it. Perfect communication between management and employees may not be realistic, but regularly speaking with employees directly can go a long way toward creating a culture of mutual respect in which good ideas flow freely. Management needs only to ask employees for their suggestions and be open to implementing the good ones.

Notes

1. K. K. Smith, "An Intergroup Perspective on Individual Behavior." In J. R. Hackman, E. E. Lawler, and L. W. Porter (eds.), *Perspectives on Behavior in Organizations* (New York: McGraw-Hill, 1977), pp. 359–372.

2. R. Rosenthal and L. Jacobson, *Pygmalion in the Classroom: Teacher Expectation and Pupils' Intellectual Development* (New York: Rinehart and Winston, 1968).

*Forty-six percent of employees believe their organizations
do not treat employees with personal respect.*

Management doesn't respect us.

A major international manufacturer of construction products asked me to help it develop an employee survey. The vice president of Human Resources asked if it would be possible to organize the survey into the same four stakeholder categories listed in the four-color glossy booklet describing the company's new vision. It was an impressive, well-organized piece, with separate pages listing how the company provided value to the community, shareholders, customers, and employees.

As a precaution, we decided to conduct a pre-test of the survey instrument to make certain employees understood how to answer each of the items and that we were asking the right questions. We invited a dozen employees to the session. They represented a cross-section of the employee population, including supervisors, hourly employees, and members of each of the major departments.

I distributed the survey and asked them to complete it. After about twenty minutes I asked, "So, what do you think?" Their responses shocked me. Each of them said, "If this survey came to my desk, I wouldn't complete it." When I asked them to explain, they told me, "This is the company's way of pushing their new vision on us rather than really caring about what we think about working here."

In short, those employees felt they were not respected. Needless to say, we redesigned the survey into categories that assessed the views of employees on the issues that most concerned them, not according to the categories of the new vision.

My sister used to work in the back office of a large health-care organization. Along with about twenty-five other college-educated employees, she was responsible for processing medical claims. Here are three memos she and her coworkers received from management. These are verbatim transcripts of the memos, including the capitalization:

> "Just a reminder to take care of all personal matters before you punch in. This includes personal hygiene, morning beverages or food, or any other personal task that is not directly work related. You should not be attending to any of these matters once you have punched in to start your work day."

> "I RESPECTFULLY ASK THAT EACH OF YOU PAY ATTENTION TO YOUR WORK, AND IF YOU SHOULD HEAR SOMEONE ELSE'S PERSONAL BUSINESS, THAT YOU IGNORE WHAT YOU HAVE HEARD."

> "DRESS CODE: THE DRESS CODE IS FOR EVERYONE TO FOLLOW . . . IF YOU ARE UNSURE WHETHER OR NOT YOUR OUTFIT MEETS THE REQUIREMENTS, IT PROBABLY DOESN'T . . . WE ARE BUSINESS CASUAL . . . IF EVEN ONE PERSON CANNOT FOLLOW THE GUIDELINES, THEN EVERYONE WILL DRESS BUSINESS."

The Problem for Employers

Memos like these are insulting, degrading, and disrespectful. If management wants employees to act as adults, they need to treat them like adults. Management cannot expect to receive respect from their employees if that respect is not reciprocated.

My work takes me into many different types of organizations. Even on an initial visit, I can typically tell whether an organization respects its employees. Here are some of the things that indicate a disrespectful work environment:

- Special parking places are reserved for senior executives of the company but not for "the employee of the month," handicapped employees, or visitors.

- Managers don't introduce their support staff or colleagues to visitors.

- Visitors are kept waiting for long periods of time in the reception area.

- The receptionist makes no attempt to make visitors feel comfortable.

- The simple words "please" and "thank you" are rarely used.

The Psychology of It All

Why does management treat employees disrespectfully? There are at least four reasons.

1. *Different Perspectives.* As previously discussed, senior management's perspective atop the organization differs from those within the organization. Uppers are generally inclined to have a dim view of the skills and knowledge of employees and don't respect them.

2. *Mirroring.* Remember, "mirroring" is the phenomenon in which relationships at the upper levels of an organization spread to lower levels. "It all starts at the top" is a truism, not a cliché. For example, if parents demonstrate violent behavior in front of their children, the children will undoubtedly express these same behaviors to others. Similarly, if senior managers don't respect their direct reports, these second-level managers will demonstrate a similar level of disrespect to *their* direct reports, and so on. The practice of disrespect

spreads, or mirrors itself, throughout the organization and becomes part of its culture.

But, you may ask, how does this disrespect begin in the first place? One reason is that uppers often experience disrespect in their external environment. Perhaps their suppliers, stockbrokers, or customers disrespect them. This then starts the process of mirroring within the organization.

3. *Insecurity.* A third reason for disrespect of employees is insecurity. Managers and supervisors who are not confident in their own skills and abilities often develop a lack of respect toward the views of their direct reports.

4. *Failure to Value Employees.* Another underlying cause of disrespect is viewing all employees as expenses rather than income-producing assets. Senior managers in healthy organizations know that the engine driving their business is their employees. They treat them as investments that must be respected. They focus on the fact that each employee represents $100,000 to $300,000 of revenue, rather than the expense of their salary and benefits.

➲ Solutions

1. Respect employee privacy.
Discuss personal and sensitive issues in private. Also, as noted in Chapter 1, don't spy on employees. A 2005 survey by the American Management Association of 526 U.S. companies found that 55 percent use some type of software to monitor their employees' incoming and outgoing e-mail.[1] Be the exception. Take the high road and respect the privacy of your employees.

2. Get to know your employees as people.
In healthy organizations, supervisors, managers, and even the senior-most executives know the names of the majority of their

employees. They also know a little about their families and major interests. Employees are more than just human machines.

3. Communicate with employees individually.
Don't send blanket e-mails that threaten or chastise all employees. Even in organizations where a high level of teamwork is important, employees must be managed individually.

4. Apply discipline to individuals, not teams.
If there is a problem with an employee's conduct, dress, or use of company time, talk to that person individually. If necessary, use the organization's performance management and discipline processes, but be above board in communicating your concerns and actions to the employee.

5. Recognize that employees have lives outside of work.
There is no excuse for blatantly abusing company time, but is receiving a periodic call from a family member really so terrible? Is checking in with a childcare provider cheating your employer? Certainly it is not.

6. Treat employees as adults.
Eating a two-hour full-course meal during work hours is probably inappropriate, but is sipping coffee or soda at your desk a violation of company time? Probably not.

7. Remember the Golden Rule.
Management should give employees the same level of respect and dignity that they would want to be shown themselves.

Conclusion

There is no excuse for management treating employees disrespectfully, but it happens all the time—and employees hate it. Employees should be treated as individuals and as valuable assets of the organization. Get to know employees personally, communicate with them individually, apply discipline to individuals not teams, recognize that employees have lives outside of work, and treat them as adults. In short, treat employees with respect and they will reciprocate that feeling toward management and the organization's goals.

Note

1. 2005 Electronic Monitoring & Surveillance Survey: "Many Companies Monitoring, Recording, Videotaping—and Firing—Employees." Study cosponsored by the American Management Association and the ePolicy Institute. Reported May 18, 2005: amanet.org/press/amanews/ems05.htm.

So who's in charge anyway?

I t was the biggest decision of his career and the biggest decision by his organization in more than a decade—and he blew it.

Grady Little, manager of the 2003 Boston Red Sox, was at the helm during the seventh and deciding game of the American League Championship Series against their nemesis for more than 80 years, "the Evil Empire": the New York Yankees. Pedro Martinez, former Cy Young award winner and the Sox's best pitcher, was on the mound.

The Sox were leading 5 to 2 in the eighth inning. The fans back in New England were cautiously optimistic that this might finally be the year to overcome the famed "curse of the Bambino." Pedro had pitched brilliantly up to this point, but his pitch count was over the magical number 100 and Grady rarely kept him in after that. Besides, the Red Sox bullpen had been performing very well in the postseason.

In the eighth inning Pedro allowed two hits, and with one out Grady came to the mound and asked his tired-armed superstar whether he wanted to stay in the game. The brave battler Martinez said, "Keep me in." As he usually did when his superstar spoke, Grady complied.

Little was barely back to his seat in the dugout when Pedro gave up a run-scoring hit, making the score 5 to 3. Still Grady remained seated. The rest is history. The fourth hit of the inning tied the game, and the Sox later lost in the bottom of the 11th inning on a crushing Bucky Dent-like home run by weak-hitting Aaron Boone. Red Sox Nation was devastated—yet again.

Why did Grady Little allow his pitcher to make this decision? Unfortunately, he relied too heavily on the input of his subordinate rather than on his own instincts or his business advisors—a big mistake.

The Problem for Employers

Managers in organizations need to know when to gather information from employees and when to make the hard decisions themselves even if it means disregarding employees. It is management's job to gather all the information, weigh this information, and then make the final decision with the best interests of the organization in mind.

When managers abdicate their decision-making responsibilities, employees lose trust in them. A lack of trust leads to lowered commitment to the organization and decreased morale.

The Psychology of It All

Part of the "psychological contract" employees implicitly accept when they join an organization is that in return for compensation and being treated fairly, they will follow the decisions made by their supervisors.

Most employees have strong opinions about what decisions should be made. They want to have input, but they would rather have management actually make the crucial decisions. They are willing to play a subservient role if management will step up to the plate and make the tough decisions. They are usually willing to follow along to implement those decisions.

When management makes the wrong decisions or fails to make decisions in a timely manner, they are violating the psychological contract.

➲ Solutions

1. Understand that the goals of the organization and the goals of your employees are not always the same.

Pedro wanted to show the world that he could continue to mow down the Yankee hitters. He wanted to silence his critics after his earlier loss in the series. He probably also wanted to make sure that his income would stay astronomically high during his upcoming salary negotiations. These, of course, were not the goals of Grady Little, who simply wanted to get five more outs and win the game. The primary input used to make this decision came from the wrong person.

2. Know where to draw the line.

Workers should certainly make many day-to-day decisions, but management should make other, more strategic decisions, alone. In Grady Little's case, the decision should have been made by him alone—without even consulting the worker. Did he really expect Pedro to say, "Yes, please take me out?"

3. Consult with senior advisors.

The decision was Grady Little's to make, but he needed to gather more input from the other coaches on the team and his catcher, Jason Varitek. Little let his emotions and the emotions of his superstar determine the decision. This is not a wise business strategy.

Conclusion

Management needs to make the hard decisions even when those decisions fly in the face of the wishes of their valued employees. They need to consult with employees and supervisors before making their decision, but employees will be happier if they know management will not hesitate to make the important tough decisions themselves.

Forty-five percent of employees don't trust the information they receive from their senior management.

I don't trust the information I receive from management.

I was consulting to a privately-held East Coast environmental engineering firm, that employed a work force of approximately 350 in ten locations in the United States and several overseas. Trust in management was at an all-time low.

In response to declining revenues, the company was in the midst of a great deal of change. During the previous year they had downsized by more than 25 percent and hired a new operations manager to help the company better focus on the bottom line. They were planning on splitting the company into a small administrative services group and a larger operations group. The owner was also considering selling the company.

Employees felt senior management knew much more about the future of the company than they were telling, and employee morale had become a major problem. The rumor mill was running rampant as employees feared the company would be sold and there would be more layoffs. They no longer trusted management to be honest with them.

The truth was that senior management had no idea what was going to happen next. They were also in the dark, and had not even developed contingency plans in the event revenue continued to decline. They did not want to alarm anyone with possible "what-if" scenarios, so they passed very little information about the situation along to employees. They didn't even admit that they too were uncertain about the future.

In another instance I conducted an employee survey for a unionized manufacturing organization with plants in Atlanta, New Jersey, and Western Massachusetts. Prior to developing the survey, I visited each plant to speak with the local managers and employees. At one of the plants, management and the employees were in constant conflict. Neither group trusted the other. This situation had been deteriorating for many years, but management felt powerless to do anything about it. No matter what they said to employees, employees did not believe them, so management stopped trusting employees. No one even remembered how the vicious cycle first got started. One manager confided, "It has gotten so bad and lasted for so long that the only way to end this terrible situation is for us to fire every employee, move the plant to a different part of the country, and hire all new employees and managers."

The Problem for Employers

I have sat in on many presentations in which senior management attempts to honestly present important information about the performance of the company to employees. It is not uncommon to see many employees sitting with their arms folded expressing their deep skepticism with their body language. How can management expect employees to align themselves with the goals of the organization when employees don't trust the information they receive about these goals? When employees don't trust the information they receive from management, employee productivity and commitment to the organization declines.

The Psychology of It All

Senior managers tend to lose sight of the fact that they have a very different perspective about the organization than do rank-and-file employees. They have access to more information about the performance of the organization, the market, and the economy. But they often ignore their important responsibility to communicate this information to employees.

Senior managers believe that if there is nothing important to report to employees, they need not communicate anything. Employees, however, are thirsty for information. When they don't receive it, they believe it is being intentionally withheld from them.

Senior managers assume that when they meet with middle managers, the important information shared at the meeting will be passed along. Unfortunately, this is often not the case. It is not uncommon for middle managers to leave a briefing of senior management and report nothing to their direct reports. They assume that employees don't really need to know the information, or they intentionally withhold it from employees. They may believe that information is power and that telling employees all they know would diminish their authority. But middle managers have the responsibility for passing along information to their employees.

Employees also may have unrealistic expectations about what information senior management should provide them. If they haven't heard something specific from management, they often assume the worst and mistakenly assume that management doesn't respect them enough to be honest with them.

➲ Solutions

1. Bypass the middlemen.
Middle managers in most organizations frequently say, "Senior managers and employees would understand each other much better if they would only communicate directly." As previously discussed, ironically, it is these "middles" that get in the way of that communication. In passing on information, people often intentionally or unintentionally filter, embellish, or put their own spin on the message.

In small organizations, senior managers can:

- Hold regular all-employee meetings
- Conduct informal breakfast or lunch meetings with employees
- Meet face-to-face with individual employees when walking through the halls

In large organizations, senior management can:

- Prepare videotaped messages
- Send e-mails or memos directly to employees
- Use the services of communication professionals to help choose the appropriate media, message, and moment

2. Differentiate between "nice-to-know" and "need-to-know."

It is important that senior managers establish criteria for what type of information should be communicated directly to employees and what should not. For example, information should be communicated directly to all employees if it:

- Affects the work they perform
- Has a personal impact upon their future within the organization
- Affects them financially

3. Communicate "don't-knows" as well as "do-knows."

Above all else, employees want honesty. It is important that management communicate what they don't know *and* what they do know. For example, they should be honest with employees when they are uncertain about:

- How the economy will influence the organization
- The possible need for layoffs
- Future plans for the direction of the organization

4. Overcommunicate.

You can never communicate important information too frequently. Management should communicate important messages to employees more than once.

5. Use multiple communication channels.

Employees have different preferences for how they receive information. Some like to read it in the company newsletter, some in an e-mail, and others at a presentation by senior managers. To effectively reach everyone, multiple methods should be used.

Conclusion

Kept in the dark, employees become unhappy. They hate management for not being open and honest with them. To maintain mutual trust, managers need to be sensitive to the need for employees to really know what is happening with the organization. You can keep employees well informed by circumventing the hierarchy, communicating directly using multiple channels, and communicating what you know and what you don't know about what is important to their work and to their future.

My boss is a terrible manager.

It was the fifth year of my graduate studies and finding a good dissertation topic had become a major challenge. My criterion was something I called the "so-what-test." I needed to be able to find a research topic that I felt passionate about because I believed it was important and worthwhile. But finding a topic that passed this test was proving to be difficult.

One day, one of my faculty advisors at the University of Maryland suggested that while I was in limbo with my dissertation I volunteer to help him with a new research project. The task was to find out why employee turnover was so high in the physical plant department of the University. I agreed to interview people who were planning to leave.

My very first interview made a long-lasting impression on me. An employee who had been on the job just six months told me, "I've never had a more miserable six months in my life." Suddenly, I had found a topic that passed my "so-what-test."

It turned out that this employee, a man in his late forties, had been a carpenter for twenty-three years prior to joining the University. A back injury had forced him to seek his current position, a desk job in which he processed maintenance work order requests. After having been self-employed for many years, this was his first foray into a full-time job within an organization.

The man cited an inability to get along with his supervisor as the major reason for his wanting to leave. He told me she was a micromanager who had very little respect for his breadth of experience. He felt unappreciated. She was also a poor communicator who spoke with him only when she had a criticism.

For my thesis I interviewed fifty recently departed employees.[1] Many explained to me that one of the major reasons they left was the difficulty they were having with their supervisors.

The Problem for Employers

Most employees experience a bad boss at least once in their career. Many actually feel they've *never* had a good boss. Insensitivity, failure to communicate, and a lack of fairness are the hallmarks of poor supervision.

Why is it that good supervisors are hard to find? Here are six reasons:

1.   *Difficulty of Supervision.* Handling the complex issues of motivating employees and solving job- and people-related problems is difficult. Few are capable of handling all these responsibilities well.

2.   *The Peter Principle.* Organizations often promote those who are good at selling and making their numbers rather than those who have demonstrated good leadership and people skills.

3.   *Poor Hiring Practices.* In this age of specialization, employers rarely focus on hiring people with good potential for supervising others. Instead, they are inclined to look only at the technical skills of applicants. Characteristics such as the ability to motivate others and to solve complex people problems, as well as emotional intelligence, are rarely considered during the hiring process.

4. *Lack of Recognition for Good Supervision.* Pay increases and promotions for supervisors are rarely based on how well they actually supervise others.

5. *Lack of Training.* Most organizations do a poor job of providing the appropriate training for their supervisors. Training is viewed as a needless expense rather than an important investment.

6. *Lack of Good Role Models.* Excellent senior-level managers who are able to mentor other managers and supervisors are the exception rather than the rule. Instead, it is often the blind leading the blind.

The Psychology of It All

Few employees can maintain their motivation and good spirits when working for someone with poor supervisory skills. The day-to-day reality of employees is defined to a large extent by their direct supervisor. Employees need to feel that they are respected, appreciated, and treated fairly.

There have been many theories developed over the years regarding the relationship between supervisory behaviors and employee satisfaction, motivation, and performance. Early theories assumed that good supervisors possess a number of universal traits that they are either born with or have learned. For example, good supervisors utilize excellent task management skills such as planning and organizing, and they have outstanding people skills such as charisma and emotional intelligence. The key for organizations is to find supervisors who already have these skills, or who have potential and can be trained.

More recent behavioral theories of supervision suggest that there are two basic styles of leadership: the task-oriented style, and the people-centered style. *Task-oriented* supervisors increase employee motivation by making it clear to employees how they can achieve valued rewards. *People-centered* supervisors increase employee motivation and satisfaction by creating a supportive environment. Both strategies can be effective.

The research of noted business theorist Robert House shows that supervisors are effective when they provide employees with the belief that if they work hard they will achieve goals, and that achieving those goals will allow them to obtain the rewards they value.[2]

At about the same time, Edwin Locke of the University of Maryland theorized that supervisors affect employee satisfaction by influencing the degree to which employees are able to attain their job *values*.[3] These include task values such as interesting and enjoyable work assignments, and non-task values such as raises, promotions, time off, and better equipment and working conditions. A good supervisor must be able to identify the values of his employees and then provide the opportunity for them to attain those values.

➲ Solutions

Good bosses possess the traits, styles, or skills that enable them to effectively provide employees with a structured and supportive environment that enables them to attain the rewards and values they desire. Here are seven basic principles for becoming a better boss.

1. Treat employees with respect and dignity.
2. Involve employees in decisions.
3. Empower employees.
4. Clearly communicate assignments.
5. Listen, listen, listen.
6. Recognize that your job includes solving "people problems."
7. Provide personal recognition.

Conclusion

Many employees are unhappy with their bosses, but being a good boss is difficult. It takes thoughtful action and a commitment to continually try new approaches to learn what is most effective for you and your employees. If you supervise others, become a student of the craft. Don't become known as "that terrible boss I had at my last job."

Notes

1. B. L. Katcher, *The Psychological Experience of Leaving a Job,* unpublished doctoral dissertation, University of Maryland, College Park, 1983.

2. R. J. House, "A Path Goal Theory of Leader Effectiveness," *Administrative Science Quarterly* 16, 3 (September 1971): 321–338.

3. E. A. Locke, "The Supervisor as 'Motivator': His Influence on Employee Performance and Satisfaction." In R. A. Steers and L. W. Porter (Eds.), *Motivation and Work Behavior* (New York: McGraw-Hill, 1975), pp. 360–372.

Part III

Employees Aren't Receiving What They Really Need

I've lost confidence in management.

O ften management is the last to know that they have lost the confidence of their employees. My first consulting contract after going out on my own in 1993 was a 70-store retail clothing store chain catering to women in need of high-end, large-size clothing. The president of the organization told me that the purpose of the survey was to help him make the organization a better place to work.

About two weeks into the program I received a call from a venture capital firm based in San Francisco. "You don't know me, but I am the head of the board of directors of your new client," said the caller. "We asked the president to have the survey conducted, so you are actually conducting it for us, not for him. Once you have completed your analysis, send the results of the survey to me directly." He then added, "Oh, and by the way, don't tell the president we have spoken."

Since the president had hired me, I sent the report separately to both the president and the head of the board. About a week later I received a call from the venture capital firm telling me that they wanted me to present the results of the survey at an emergency meeting of the board. A few minutes before the meeting, the head of the board came into the room to tell me, "I just want you to know that this morning we accepted the president's resignation."

I probably should have expected this, but I was shocked. My services had clearly been used to show the board that the workforce had lost confidence in the president. In most organizations, the fact that employees have little or no confidence in senior management is an accepted fact of life. In this case, it led to the president's dismissal.

The Problem for Employers

Our nation has been suffering for many years from an erosion of confidence in our business institutions. The fact that more than half of all employees believe their organization is not well managed is not surprising, given the following facts:

- Huge numbers of employees have lost their jobs due to layoffs.

- There has been a rash of sobering news about management improprieties at previously well-respected companies, such as MCI WorldCom, Enron, and Tyco.

- Large numbers of employees have seen their once-valuable stock options become worthless.

- Pension programs in many organizations have failed.

Employees with little confidence in management develop a cynical view of their employment situation. Although they may take pride in their work and enjoy their relationships with coworkers, they are unable to maintain enthusiasm and faithfulness to the organization.

The Psychology of It All

Employees agree to surrender their time and energy in exchange for pay, benefits, and management providing a comfortable working environment and a viable business. When employees believe that management is not making good decisions for the company, they feel that the unwritten psychological contract with their employer has been violated. They therefore reconsider their own willingness to commit their time and energy to the organization.

➲ Solutions

1. Produce results.

Most importantly, employees want to know that someone is doing a good job of minding the store. Just like stockholders, they want to see tangible results, an honest accounting of the organization's financial condition, and well-conceived plans for the future.

2. Share the wealth.

Employees can be quite accepting of hefty senior management salaries if they feel that they too are sharing in the success and growth of the organization. When business is good, it is time to institute profit-sharing programs and enhance raises and bonuses.

3. Recognize that you are accountable to employees.

In many organizations, senior managers have forgotten that they are accountable to employees as well as to stockholders and customers.

4. Be honest with your employees.

Employees can live with slumps in the business. They can also live with a year without bonuses or raises. What they cannot and should not tolerate is management's insincerity and dishonesty. Communicate successes *and* failures.

Conclusion

It is important to employees to be able to maintain confidence in management's ability to successfully lead the organization. Employees resent management when it doesn't live up to their end of the bargain. They will have more confidence in the decisions made by management if you openly communicate with them and treat them as true business partners.

Fifty-eight percent of employees say their department is shorthanded.

We're understaffed.

A large insurance company in New England surveyed the employees of a smaller company they had recently acquired in Maryland.
This 200-person acquisition had a long, proud history of serving its
local market. Most of their employees had been with the company for
many years.

The survey found that employees believed their hard work was
responsible for the growth the company had experienced during the
previous few years. They also were concerned they were understaffed.
However, based on available staffing level studies in the industry, they
were actually overstaffed. These employees had grown accustomed to
a relatively light workload but still felt overworked. Management's dilemma was how to address employee concerns without increasing
their payroll costs.

The Problem for Employers

Our research shows that the majority of employees believe there are
not enough qualified employees to handle the work in their department. Here are some reasons why employees feel overworked:

The Staff Is Slow to Adapt to Changing Technology

For this company in Maryland, employees were slow to adjust to the new technology their new parent had introduced. They had been using outdated manual procedures and lacked the computer savvy to quickly adapt to the new systems. As a result, they felt understaffed. What was really needed was not more staff, but better training or different employees who were more suited to using new technology.

Change or Die

Organizations must continuously adapt to the changing needs of their customers in order to survive. For example, a Web-based Internet commerce company helped small businesses establish shopping carts on their websites. Its business model required that the process of acquiring new customers and servicing them should be 95 percent automated. But the customer satisfaction survey we conducted for them revealed that customers wanted more personal attention, not more on-screen documentation or Web pages containing answers to frequently asked questions.

The desires of their customers forced their well-compensated sales staff to perform double-duty as customer service agents. Because the only way they could attract and retain new merchants was by providing time-consuming handholding, their sales staff spent more and more time servicing customers and less time finding new ones. In short, they didn't have the right staffing for their new business model.

Demand Often Changes Faster Than Supply

An office manager of a large, busy medical group practice is responsible for five office workers who handle medical records and the paperwork required by the insurance companies.

One day the senior partner told her they would be adding a new physician to the practice. She also learned that one of their larger HMOs was changing their procedures so she would now be required to complete additional paperwork for each patient. She knew she would need more staff, but to hire and train them would take months. Her existing staff was already overtaxed.

Staff Cuts Go Too Far

Declining revenue forced one company to impose a 10 percent layoff. To be fair, they decided to implement an across-the-board layoff strategy. Each department was required to reduce their staff count by one. Not surprisingly, an employee survey of "the survivors" found that this strategy created a particular workload problem in the smallest departments because they lost a greater percentage of their employees.

Required Skills Change

One financial service company has many dedicated, tenured employees. To improve efficiency, it gradually upgraded their internal systems. Many functions previously performed by hand were now fully automated. Our employee survey found that as a result, the technical staff felt overworked and the old-timers felt underutilized. What they now needed were fewer do-it-by-hand employees and more programmers and computer-savvy workers. The company's required skills had changed.

The Psychology of It All

Employees gradually reach a comfort level with the amount of work they are expected to perform for the compensation they receive. Either reducing the compensation or asking employees to perform more work for the same compensation can disrupt this delicate balance. According to equity theory, when this happens, employees become unhappy and want to restore the balance by either reducing their workload or receiving more pay.

There are no rules regarding the amount of work one should perform for a certain level of pay. While market forces determine pay levels, employees develop an unconscious perception about the appropriate amount of effort they should expend. It is as if they have an internal scale that weighs the amount of work they perform versus the compensation they receive. Employers must be aware that employees are sensitive to changes in this balance.

➲ Solutions

It is unlikely that the flow of work will remain at a constant level throughout the year or from year to year. Yet this is what employees expect. Here are a few suggestions for handling this problem:

1. Set realistic expectations.
Make it clear to employees when they are hired, and then periodically afterwards, that their workload will depend upon the needs of the business and its customers. Tell them they should expect to be busier during certain times of the year than others.

2. Ask employees about the workload.
Employees are often the best source of preliminary information about the need for more or better-qualified staff. Simply ask them their opinions through confidential interviews and employee surveys. Realize, of course, that their desire for more staff may be more self-serving than reflective of a real need.

3. Conduct periodic staffing audits.
Staffing levels don't necessarily match the needs of a changing company. A systematic audit of the volume of work to be performed and the needed skills can identify any mismatches. An objective outsider should be used to conduct this analysis.

4. Retrain staff.
Many organizations talk about retraining staff, but few actually do it. Once an audit identifies shortages in skills, retraining of existing staff can often fill the gap.

5. Use relief employees.

When I was a camper during the summers, counselors took one day off per week. The day our counselor was off, a relief counselor took his place. Organizations should maintain a cadre of relief workers that can cover when employees are out due to sickness or vacation. These relief workers can also help out when additional staff is needed to handle occasional increases in workload in certain departments.

Conclusion

Employees resent management when they feel overworked or understaffed. Real or imagined, employee concerns about their workload are often unavoidable. But there are measures that employers can take to better manage these concerns. Avoiding the problem is not one of them. Set realistic expectations about workload, conduct periodic staffing audits, be open to retraining staff, use relief workers, and ask employees how they feel about their workload. Most importantly, make certain that understaffing is not adversely affecting customer satisfaction.

❶❸

Forty-seven percent of all employees say they don't receive the information they need to do their job well.

They don't tell me what I need to know to do my work.

A pharmaceutical firm, a division of a Fortune 100 chemical company, took its orders directly from its parent. The researchers at the pharmaceutical firm were working on several experimental drugs. Their job was to conduct animal drug testing and work their way through all the many FDA procedures for gaining approvals.

Each experiment required months of painstaking preparation, followed by additional months of rigorous research. The problem was that the parent company kept changing their minds about what drugs they wanted them to test and how they wanted the tests to be conducted. This left the researchers extremely frustrated. They were constantly stopping, starting, and restarting their experiments. Our employee survey revealed that more than two-thirds felt they weren't receiving the information they needed to do their jobs well.

In another situation, a large gas utility, which had grown steadily through the years and had offices throughout New England, had problems with their internal information systems. They were outdated and not built for the utility's large size. The field repairmen would receive service orders several days late that were often incomplete or just plain wrong. Employees were constantly frustrated by the organization's poor information flow. For example, the marketing department sent

85

out a huge mailing to millions of customers about new service offerings only to learn too late that the services were not yet ready. In fact, an employee survey revealed that 70 percent felt they weren't receiving the information they needed to do their job well.

The Problem for Employers

When employees feel that they are not receiving the information they need to do their job well, they become frustrated and the quality of the organization's products and services suffers. Below are some of the key employee questions that frequently go unanswered:

- *To Management*: What organizational and marketplace changes are taking place that will affect our jobs? What are the priorities?

- *To Supervisors*: What exactly do you want me to do? What is my budget? When do you need the work to be completed? How well am I doing? What should I be doing differently?

- *To Coworkers*: When will the work I need from you be completed? What are your expectations of me?

- *To Customers*: How satisfied are you with the products and services we provide? What would you like us to do differently?

The Psychology of It All

There are a number of reasons why this information is not forthcoming:

1. *Unnecessary Secrecy*. Management often mistakenly assumes that by withholding information they will be able to retain power and influence over employees.

2. *Ineffective Supervision*. Although communication is the most critically important supervisory skill, many supervisors enter the ranks

of management because of their technical expertise, not their people skills.

3. *Communication Not Built into the Workflow System.* Organizations typically do a better job of planning the flow of materials and products than they do planning the flow of information. Critical information often slips through the cracks.

4. *Lack of a Cooperative Spirit.* Without a strong spirit of cooperation, employees are more apt to withhold rather than share important information.

5. *Information Simply Not Available.* Employees often mistakenly assume that information is available but that it is being intentionally withheld from them.

➲ Solutions

1. Conduct an information-needs analysis.

A systematic analysis should be conducted for each job in the organization that identifies what information is needed, when, and from whom. The results of this analysis then must be fully integrated into the organization's daily procedures.

2. Squelch secrecy.

Encourage openness. Without a good ethical, privacy, or legal rationale, secrecy within organizations is counterproductive and should be eliminated.

3. Provide customer satisfaction information.

Customer satisfaction surveys should be conducted on an ongoing basis. The information obtained from these studies should be communicated to all employees, especially those with customer contact.

4. Conduct the JFK exercise.

During John F. Kennedy's inaugural address, he said, "Ask not what your country can do for you, ask what you can do for your country." Similarly, employees should develop a list *not* of information that they need FROM others in the organization, but of the information they can provide FOR others. If everyone adopts this mindset, there will be a strong flow of communication throughout the organization.

5. Focus on the communication skills of supervisors.

The ability to effectively pass the appropriate information to others is a critically important supervisory skill. It should be one of the most important factors in the hiring and promotion of supervisors.

Conclusion

Employees resent management and are less productive when they don't receive the information they need to perform their work. Organizations need to take proactive measures to make certain employees receive the information necessary to do their jobs well. They should conduct an information-needs analysis, squelch secrecy, provide customer satisfaction information, encourage each individual to improve communication with others in the organization, and hire and promote supervisors on the basis of their communication skills.

❶❹

We need more training.

During the frenzied dot-com boom of the late 1990s I was consulting to a 140-employee venture capital-backed Internet service company. It was able to hire top-notch programmers only by offering them stock options, a nice office, a generous salary, and a rich benefit package.

Many of the programmers, however, complained that they weren't receiving the training they needed to do their work. The technology was changing rapidly and they were not given the opportunity to attend training programs or engage in any professional development activities. These programmers felt that the key to their own personal success within the company and in their careers was to stay current with the latest programming languages. They knew that an out-of-date programmer was worthless in the market and doomed for career stagnation.

But the company was struggling to stay afloat, and needed every programmer to be 100 percent billable. The last thing management felt it could afford was the cost of sending employees to training programs. But employees grew increasingly unhappy about their lack of training.

The Problem for Employers

Organizations spend a huge portion of their operating budgets compensating employees. In return, they expect them to provide excellent products and services to their customers. Yet half of all employees say they don't receive the training they need to do their job well, mainly because:

- Many organizations view training as a frivolous fringe benefit, rather than a vital business investment.

- Senior management doesn't believe training programs are effective.

- Training professionals don't do a good job of demonstrating to senior management that investing in training yields tangible results.

Here's why employers need their employees to continue to learn new skills:

1. *Capital Improvement.* Organizations spend millions of dollars to upgrade their plants and equipment, yet precious little on upgrading their most important asset: their human capital. Besides, if employees don't receive continuous training, the most up-to-date equipment will not be used to its fullest capability.

2. *Morale Improvement.* Employees who continuously upgrade their job skills will also continuously improve their productivity. Happy employees may be more productive, but more productive employees are also happier.

3. *Ability to Adapt to Change.* The more skilled the workforce, the easier it will be for the entire organization to adapt to changes in the demand for its products and services.

The Psychology of It All

For a variety of psychological and practical reasons employees want to continue to learn and grow. Abraham Maslow's theory regarding what he called the "hierarchy of needs" suggests that all employees are motivated to self-actualize (i.e., become all that they are capable of becoming).[1] Doing so requires them to continually develop their skills and knowledge.

The "Two-Factor Theory of Job Motivation," originally developed by Frederick Herzberg and his colleagues in 1957, posited that all job factors can be classified into two categories based upon whether they contribute primarily to job satisfaction or dissatisfaction.[2] His theory suggests that employees are more satisfied on their jobs if they are challenged and provided with the opportunity to grow.

Systems theory would suggest that all employees must proactively manage their careers in a rapidly changing and evolving system. Just as in nature, the Darwinian principle of "survival of the fittest" applies here too. Employees must continually learn and upgrade their knowledge, skills, and abilities in order to survive in the rapidly changing and turbulent economy. They are, therefore, motivated to continuously improve.

➲ Solutions

1. Communicate the importance of learning.

Management should communicate to employees that their organization is a learning center. Providing resources and encouragement for employees to continually upgrade their skills will help attract and retain a dedicated work force.

2. Show them the money.

Establish a personnel development fund that gives each employee a set amount of money each year (e.g., $250) that can be used for any job-related learning activity, such as professional meetings, books, or videos. Also, provide tuition reimbursement to enable employees to take college courses in their field.

3. Provide opportunities to visit customers.
Face time with customers will help employees gain a better understanding of their needs.

4. Institute a job rotation program.
Develop a system whereby employees rotate between jobs. This will help upgrade their skills and give them a better understanding of the relationships among different jobs within the organization.

5. Institute a shadowing program.
A program in which employees are given the opportunity to closely observe other workers will allow them to understand and appreciate other jobs throughout the organization.

6. Provide a resource center.
Establish a center and stock it with job-related books, technical manuals, industry periodicals, and training videos. Allow employees to visit the center on company time.

7. Systematically assess training needs.
The job skills required to be successful are constantly evolving because of changes in technology and customer needs. Carefully conducted "training needs assessments" will identify gaps in employee skills. The organization can then focus on what type of training employees really need.

8. Evaluate training programs.
Unfortunately, only a very small percentage of training programs are ever systematically evaluated. To do so requires:

- Identifying the objectives of the training program
- Establishing a baseline measure prior to the training
- Comparing the before and after results

If, for example, your objective is to increase customer satisfaction by improving the telephone skills of your staff, only by comparing the before and after customer satisfaction results will it become clear whether the effort was successful. Without such studies, senior management often feels that they are just wasting their money on training. An evaluation study offers proof one way or the other.

The importance of evaluating training programs was brought home to me while consulting to a financial services company. This company spent millions of dollars developing informational materials for meetings in which its financial experts taught employees at other companies how to save for retirement using the 401(k) plan managed by the company. The goal of the workshop was to give employees information that would help them feel comfortable enrolling in the retirement program. The company needed to know whether employees were learning anything and whether the program was increasing the likelihood that they would rollover their retirement savings into the program. By having the employees answer questions both before and after the enrollment meetings about their knowledge of such financial concepts as compound interest and before-tax savings, the company was able to improve the usefulness of the meetings.

9. Invest in training during down periods.

Managers should change their mindset from considering training as an expense to viewing it as an important investment. Training budgets are often the first to be cut during challenging economic times, but it actually makes more sense to focus on training during a lull in business. When business is slow, employees are more able to take time from their work to attend training sessions.

10. Encourage employees to be honest about their needs.
Employees have a tendency to say they don't need training even if they know they really do. Employees need to take responsibility to say to their supervisors, "I need training and here's why."

11. Use methods other than classroom instruction.
Traditional classroom instruction is often not the best way to teach job skills. Hands-on or computer-assisted instruction, Web-based training, and audio or video training are some of the many techniques that enable individuals to work at their own pace and learn more efficiently than they would in a classroom setting.

12. Make certain that supervisors support the transfer of training.
Very often supervisors discourage and even chastise employees for using the new skills that they were taught in training programs. In that case, it's no wonder that those skills are not used. Supervisors must remain open to the idea that employees can change and grow.

Conclusion

Employees sincerely want to perform their jobs well and want to make certain they maintain marketable skills. They resent management for not providing them with the training they need. Employers need to view training programs as an investment rather than an expense.

Notes

1. A. H. Maslow, *Motivation and Personality* (New York: Harper, 1954).
2. F. Herzberg et al., *Job Attitudes: Review of Research and Opinion* (Pittsburgh: Psychological Service of Pittsburgh, 1957).

The quality of our products and services is terrible.

A t a manufacturer of welded brass fittings for large water pipes, employees in the shop complained to me, "We have a daily quota, but sometimes the raw materials we receive have defects, and other times our machinery breaks down. When that happens, the only way to meet our quota is to ship inferior products. But when we complain to management, they tell us to keep our mouths shut and ship the products anyway."

At another company, a think tank that produces research reports for the telecommunications industry costing thousands of dollars for an annual subscription, employees were concerned that the reports weren't as timely or as useful as they used to be. They worried that some of their customers would realize this and cancel their subscriptions.

Similarly, employees on the manufacturing floor of an adhesive products company complained that due to quality problems, they were receiving an excessive number of customer returns. Processing the returns was very time-consuming and was angering customers, who blamed the company for sacrificing quality to save money.

These are three examples of employees being properly concerned about the quality of the products and services their organizations provide to their customers. Back in the 1980s, when the continuous quality improvement initiatives of many organizations were catching fire and when W. Edwards Deming was the organizational guru of the day, the results of many employee surveys revealed a surprising finding. Employee ratings of the quality of the products and services produced by their own organizations were declining, not improving. This was especially true in those organizations that had devoted a great deal of time and attention to improving quality. How could this be?

The answer is that employees had become highly sensitized. By attending quality improvement classes, learning about Six Sigma, and serving on quality improvement teams, everywhere they looked they saw opportunities to improve quality. Although quality was actually improving, employees had become much more aware and critical.

Although quality has rightly become a key organizational goal at most companies, many employees have actually become *too* critical of their organizations. In the frenzy to improve quality and achieve perfection, some employees have become so focused on identifying and solving problems that they have lost sight of the fact that their customers are, for the most part, satisfied. This is often because they have little direct personal contact with customers and thus don't know how customers really feel. Since these employees spend the majority of their time solving problems and putting out fires, they don't understand that the overwhelming majority of their customers are satisfied and will continue to do business with the firm.

The Problem for Employers

Needless to say, organizations won't survive long if their customers are consistently dissatisfied with their products and services. They will also be in trouble with their employees, who in order to stay motivated need to believe that management is committed to quality. If employees believe management doesn't really care, they ask themselves, "Why should I care?"

This could result in a downward spiral of declining quality, poor customer service, and lost business.

The Psychology of It All

Leon Festinger's theory of *cognitive dissonance* suggests that individuals become frustrated and uncomfortable when there are inconsistencies between their attitudes and behaviors. If they believe that producing high quality work is important but know their own work is not, they will experience cognitive dissonance. This theory predicts that people will be motivated to reduce the dissonance by changing their behavior (e.g., improving the quality of their work or quitting their job) or by changing their attitude (e.g., the quality of the work doesn't really matter or their work quality is really not that bad).[1]

Employees want to be able to take pride in the quality of their work and the work of their organization. They want to hold their heads up high when they talk to others about what their organization stands for. Although they may not feel that their work is saving the world, they at least want to believe that they are working for an organization where everyone strives to do the best job possible for their customers. When employees feel the quality of the products and services provided to customers is low, organizational pride, that thin glue that holds many organizations together, begins to lose its grip.

⊃ Solutions

Legitimate Concerns
When employee concerns about quality are legitimate, it is critically important that management responds appropriately, as shown in the following three guidelines:

1. Investigate the problem.
Employees need to know that management will take immediate steps to investigate and act on their concerns about quality.

2. Communicate and demonstrate a commitment to quality.

Management needs to consistently let employees know the importance of providing their customers with high quality products and services. This mantra must be repeated over and over again.

3. Admit that there is a problem.

Tell the truth. Don't falsely deny that there are quality problems. Employees will usually be the first to know anyway. Honesty is the best policy. Thank employees for their concerns and admit when management has made poor decisions, bought bad raw materials, or established ineffective procedures.

Unwarranted Concerns

Sometimes, of course, employee perceptions about quality are inaccurate. Managers are often perplexed when they learn that 50 percent or more of their employees rate the quality of their products and services as poor, despite data that clearly demonstrates a high level of repeat business, low customer turnover, and high levels of customer satisfaction. Here are five possible approaches.

1. Provide employees with customer satisfaction data.

Our surveys show that 60 percent of employees do not feel they receive the customer satisfaction information they need to perform their jobs well. Customer satisfaction surveys should be conducted on a regular basis, and the results should be shared with employees. Also share data about compliments received and new orders placed, as well as about returns, errors, and complaints.

2. Identify what is important to customers.

Employees often focus their energies on improving what is most important to them, rather than on what is most important to their customers. Sharing with employees the results of surveys that identify what is most important to customers can help correctly focus their energies.

3. Track trends in customer satisfaction.
It is important for you and your employees to know whether customer satisfaction is improving, remaining constant, or declining. This information will help determine whether the organization's commitment to quality is working.

4. Provide competitive intelligence.
It can be enlightening to employees to learn how customers feel about their company's products and services compared to those provided by the competition. This information can be gathered through customer satisfaction surveys, market research studies, and by interviewing former customers of competing organizations.

5. Provide an appropriately balanced picture.
Care should be taken not to sugarcoat or distort data about customer satisfaction. Armed with accurate and complete data, you and your employees will be able to develop the appropriate perspective about actions that can be taken.

Conclusion

Employees blame management when they feel their organization is not producing quality products and services. Your first step should be to determine whether there are really quality problems or whether it is only a problem in perception. If problems do exist, provide your people with the support they need to make improvements. Even more importantly, listen to what your customers have to say about quality and communicate this information to your employees.

Note

1. L. Festinger, *Theory of Cognitive Dissonance* (Stanford: Stanford University Press, 1957).

Only 46 percent of all employees feel cooperation is good between departments.

I receive poor service from other departments.

During a series of focus groups for a New England financial services organization, employees complained about the poor customer service they receive from other departments. Everyone was pointing fingers. An internal customer satisfaction survey identified which departments were actually the culprits.

The survey contained two sections. In the first section, all employees were asked how they felt about the customer service they were *receiving* from the fifty other departments in the organization. In the second section, they were asked to rate the level of customer service they felt they were *providing* to each of the other departments.

It turned out that employees in every department felt that their department was providing much better service than their internal customers felt they were receiving from them.

The Problem for Employers

Can an organization really expect to provide excellent service to its external customers when their employees don't believe they are receiving good customer service from other departments within the organization? For example, if the sales and production departments don't cooperate with each other, customers won't receive what they were promised. Also, if the IT department doesn't cooperate with the rest of the organization, timely service to customers will suffer.

Organizations spend a great deal of time trying to increase external customer satisfaction, but very little on improving internal customer satisfaction. Although most employees are usually totally unaware of how they themselves are contributing to the problem, they typically complain that:

- Other departments don't provide them with what they need in a timely manner.

- Other departments don't understand what they do.

- They are not treated with respect and dignity by their co-workers.

- Other employees are often moody and unpleasant.

The Psychology of It All

Our research has shown that although employees generally have a high regard for their coworkers in their own work group, they often view employees in other departments as lazy, ineffective, and intentionally uncooperative.

One explanation is the phenomenon of "ethnocentrism," the belief that your own group is superior to other groups. Right or wrong, this natural human predisposition interferes with effective teamwork.

A related phenomenon that explains why work groups don't cooperate well with each other is "stereotyping." For example, sales employees often stereotype production employees as people just putting in their time with little regard for the customer. When a production problem takes place, the sales force is quick to view production employees as incompetent without really understanding the situation. Similarly, production employees stereotype sales employees as self-centered and interested only in their sales bonuses, with little understanding of how the products are really made.

Employees form these stereotypes of other work groups due, in part, to the interpersonal behavior phenomenon best explained by "attribution theory." Social psychologists Edward Jones and Richard Nisbett demonstrated that there is a fundamental difference in how people view their own behavior and the behavior of others. Individuals typically view their own behavior as being caused by the *situation,* but view the behavior of others as caused by their *disposition.*[1]

For example, if you learn that a fellow student just flunked a test, you would be naturally predisposed to judge that person as unintelligent. But the student who flunked the test would be more likely to blame the poor grade on the fact that he didn't study enough, was sick the night before the test, didn't care about the test, or that the test was poorly designed.

In the workplace, production employees might view manufacturing problems as caused by the poor quality of the raw materials they received, poorly maintained equipment, or the pressure from management to ship as much finished product each day as possible regardless of quality. They likely would not view the problem as being due to their own ineffectiveness or lack of regard for customers. Likewise, the natural tendency of sales employees might be to make a dispositional attribution by blaming the problem on the laziness and uncaring attitudes of production department employees.

These tendencies to attribute the behavior of others to something negative about their personality or attitudes are counterproductive. It would be much better for all involved if, for example, salespeople really understood the situation facing production workers and vice versa. In this way each group would be more willing to try to develop solutions to the problem rather than just shaking their heads and saying, "Those other employees are really bad."

➲ Solutions

1. Provide employee internships within the organization.
Many employees have no idea what the employees in other departments do. Although they are quick to judge their performance,

they don't understand the work others perform, how they operate, or the pressures they experience. Allowing employees to serve as interns for a few days in other departments will enable employees to better understand the work of other departments and to help them view the employees there as real people rather than merely incompetent adversaries.

2. Reverse the finger pointing.

Instead of blaming others, employees must learn to critically examine how their own actions are contributing to problems. Each time employees point a finger, ask them what *they* can do to help resolve the issue.

It's like that old story about the difference between heaven and hell. A man visits hell and sees a group of frustrated people sitting around a large dinner table. They are trying to eat their dinner but are struggling to feed themselves because their forks are each five feet long. The man next visits heaven, where people at a large table are also trying to eat using five-foot-long forks. But they have no problem because they are using their long forks to feed someone else on the other side of the table.

3. Conduct an internal customer satisfaction survey.

The survey should ask employees how they feel about the timeliness, professionalism, and quality of the services they are receiving from others in the organization. It should also include questions about the quality of the services they feel they are providing to others. I guarantee the results will be a real eye-opener to many, because they will identify specific areas of the company where internal customer service is in need of improvement.

4. Conduct the JFK exercise.

Meet with each department separately and facilitate a brainstorming session focused on developing ideas about what they can do to improve their service to other departments.

5. **Identify the best practices.**

Some employees and departments do a better job of satisfying their internal customers than others. Identify good behaviors and teach others in the organization to copy them.

Conclusion

Employees are often unhappy about the lack of cooperation they feel they receive from other departments. They blame management for creating this difficult situation. The underlying causes are ethnocentrism, stereotyping, and dispositional attributions. Organizational cooperation can be improved by instituting job rotation, reversing finger pointing, conducting internal customer satisfaction surveys, focusing departments on what they can do to improve cooperation, and identifying and mimicking best practices within your organization.

Note

1. E. E. Jones and R. E. Nisbett, "The Actor and the Observer: Divergent Perceptions of the Causes of Behavior." In Attribution: *Perceiving the Causes of Behavior* (New York: General Learning Press, 1971).

There's too much red tape here.

While trying to help a small food manufacturer improve the efficiency of their operation, I observed one of the machine operators jotting down numbers every 15 minutes in a notebook. I asked her why she was doing this. She told me she didn't know, but that several years ago her boss, who was no longer with the company, had asked her to keep the log. I asked her if anyone ever looked at the notebook and she told me, "Not that I know of."

Many bureaucratic procedures are perpetuated for no good reason. They sap the time and energy of employees. Some organizations seem to have a form, a procedure, and a rule for everything. You can't blow your nose without having to fill out a requisition or get an approval.

As an outside consultant, I often bump up against these bureaucracies when I submit my proposals or invoices. It provides me with a good understanding of what it's like for insiders in some organizations.

I frequently consult to a large manufacturer of metal products. This company has been in business for many years and has developed a bureaucracy that rivals that of the federal government. When I submitted a proposal to conduct some work for this organization, their legal department sent me a 30-page document written in legalese.

When I called purchasing to ask for an explanation, they told me, "We don't understand it either, just sign it."

As every consultant knows, sometimes bureaucracies make it very difficult to get paid. One client of mine has a 25-step approval process for all invoices. One time I actually drove 45 minutes to a facility with about 200 people whose sole job was to process invoices. I somehow found the right person and stood at her desk until she handed me a check.

Red tape is not limited to large organizations. A few years back I consulted to a small liberal arts college. Most of the faculty had been working there for many years and were tenured. It was a highly political environment. The faculty and the administration didn't trust each other. The organization was paralyzed. No one was able to make a decision about anything. Faculty committees would make recommendations for hiring a new secretary, but the recommendation had to be submitted to department chairs for approval and then to the deans. The deans would have to submit it to the president, who would need to consult with the Board of Directors. The process, even for a very simple decision, sometimes took years.

The Problem for Employers

Employees often feel it is just too difficult to get things done in their organization. Even simple activities like ordering supplies or requesting a computer repair are monumentally difficult tasks. There are just too many forms to fill out, approvals to gather, channels to pass through, or consensus-gathering meetings to conduct. The result: annoyance, frustration, and paralysis. Often employees throw up their aims in disgust and give up.

What causes this red tape in the first place, and how is it allowed to fester? Here are five reasons:

1. *Creation of New Systems as Companies Grow.* When small organizations become larger, new systems, policies, and procedures are

introduced to regulate and discipline the organization. These well-intentioned measures are supposed to help the organization operate more efficiently.

2. *Compliance.* In highly regulated organizations, such as insurance companies or banks, internal rules and procedures develop to keep the organization in compliance with new regulations and laws.

3. *The Desire for Internal Consistency.* Organizations believe that it is important to maintain consistency about how money is spent, how people are hired, and the work hours, pay levels, and dress codes of employees.

4. *Power Grabbing.* Red tape also evolves in organizations because senior management wants to maintain as much power as possible. They are under the mistaken assumption that the more power is centralized, the more efficient and productive the organization will be. But this is rarely the case. The most powerful organizations are those where employees all share power. They are unencumbered by red tape. When hundreds or thousands of people are empowered, the resulting energy of the organization is much greater than when just a few at the top are in total control.

5. *Lack of Trust.* Many organizations don't trust their employees to make decisions or to act wisely. As a result, they impose rules and approval processes to make certain employees are properly controlled and the organization operates efficiently.

These bureaucratic procedures put a stranglehold on the organization, reduce efficiency, encourage rule breaking, and foster an environment in which employees feel powerless to get anything accomplished. Red tape bogs down the organization in its own internal procedures rather than focusing on such key goals as customer satisfaction and profitability.

The Psychology of It All

The *Merriam-Webster Dictionary* defines red tape as, "Official routine or procedure marked by excessive complexity which results in delay or inaction." Its etymology is from the 1700s in England, where red tape was used to bind bulky stacks of legal documents.

When employees blindly follow official routines, procedures, and directives they often feel powerless and become paralyzed. They become reluctant to make decisions, take risks, or engage in any actions that would help the organization. Worse, they may fail to use good judgment, relying instead on rules or orders that they receive from their superiors.

In 1961, Yale University professor Stanley Milgram demonstrated the problems that can occur when employees merely comply with instructions they are given by those in authority. He set up a simple experiment in which ordinary citizens controlled an electronic shock device and were asked to shock a stranger sitting in another room. A surprising 65 percent of the subjects blindly complied with the experimenter's orders and applied high doses of electricity to the other person, not realizing that the victim was an actor and was not actually being shocked.[1] This well-known psychological study speaks to the underlying psychology of what happens when people become accustomed to blindly following procedures and orders. They can easily end up doing things that are not in the best interest of their company or customers.

While admittedly this is an extreme example of what can happen when people blindly comply with authority, it illustrates the fact that bureaucratic red tape can be destructive in organizations. Employees, without thinking, can perform acts that violate moral judgment and common sense. This blind obedience can also lead to work inefficiency, quality problems, and customer dissatisfaction.

➲ Solutions

1. Untangle the red tape.

Take a hard look at those processes that are bogging things down and frustrating employees. Are they really necessary? What damage would occur by streamlining or simplifying them? Involve those most affected in developing a set of questions to systematically evaluate these red-tape traps. For example, ask them and yourself:

- Is this policy, procedure, or practice absolutely necessary?
- Can it be simplified?
- Is there a less complex but equally effective alternative?

2. Circumvent the red tape.

Ever notice that some people in your organization just don't have the same red tape problems as you? Often this is because they have delegated red tape tasks to others. Or these red-tape avoiders just don't worry about the same approvals, forms, and protocols that others in the organization obsess about. Be bold! Don't assume the worst. Try it and see what happens; you may be pleasantly surprised.

3. Eliminate the red tape.

Organizations typically do a much better job of creating red tape than they do of eliminating it. Perhaps that form, procedure, or approval has outlived its usefulness and should be abandoned. Be a pioneer by taking the lead. Instead of streamlining operations by eliminating people, eliminate the procedures that make the people less productive.

Conclusion

Employees hate red tape and they blame management for it. It makes them powerless to use good judgment and can lead to inefficiency, quality problems, and customer dissatisfaction. Organizations need to focus on untangling, circumventing, or eliminating it.

Note

1. S. Milgram, "Behavioral study of obedience," *Journal of Abnormal and Social Psychology* 67 (1974): 371–378.

① ⑧

Sixty-one percent of employees believe their organization tolerates poor performers.

Why don't they get rid of all of the deadwood around here?

E mployees at a small, rural community hospital complained incessantly about poor performers. They felt that the organization was too tolerant of ineffective performers and should be firing them. Nurses complained that some of their colleagues were constantly coming to work late, calling in sick, and not pitching in to help. Housekeepers said that some of their coworkers only completed about half as much work as they did during a typical day. Many also felt that several of the department managers were just not doing their job.

The employees wondered, "Doesn't senior management see the problems with these employees? Are they blind?" Privately, they also questioned whether management noticed their own *good* performance.

The hospital prided itself on its friendly, congenial atmosphere. It was the kind of place where once employees took a job, they might stay the rest of their career. The majority of the staff had been with the hospital for twenty years or more. Firing someone was not only taking their job away from them, but also ostracizing them within a close-knit community.

Management was not blind. They knew there were ineffective performers within the ranks who had been tolerated for many years. But

113

they feared that taking strong action might destroy the collegial atmosphere that made the work environment so special. They also lacked the appropriate paper trail to dismiss poor performers without facing potential legal problems.

The Problem for Employers

Every organization has poor performers. I'm talking about employees who do the bare minimum. They don't break any company rules and they don't make any blatant or costly mistakes. They are nevertheless extremely harmful to the organization.

Managers who allow poor performers to just coast risk being perceived by other employees as indecisive and ineffective. They also will alienate good performers who believe management doesn't have a clue as to who is performing well and who is not. Typical complaints from these employees are:

- "Why should I work hard if my coworkers get by on less?"

- "I should be making more money than people who work less hard."

- "I have to work harder because I end up doing other people's work as well as my own."

The Psychology of It All

Equity theory predicts that when employees perceive inequity in the workplace, they will do one of the following:

- Reduce their input by exerting less effort on the job.

- Increase their outcomes by lobbying for a raise or promotion.

- Increase the poor performer's inputs by somehow rationalizing that the poor performer is actually contributing to the organization in some other way.

- Reduce the poor performer's outcomes by trying to get their coworker fired.
- Leave their job.

➲ Solutions

Parting ways with poor performers may be the best solution when no other option is possible. It can signal to other employees that poor performance is not tolerated. However, there are other options for dealing with ineffective performers that should be carefully considered first.

First Options

1. **Identify the root cause of the problem.**
Schedule a time to meet with the employee to discuss the situation. Don't wait until the annual performance review. Try to identify what is causing the performance problem and whether it can be improved. Explore potential causes both inside and outside the workplace. Most importantly, make the employee a partner in identifying possible solutions.

2. **Assign the employee to a different supervisor.**
Sometimes a different supervisor may be able to bring out the best from a low performing employee. A fresh start may be all that is needed.

3. **Place the employee in a different position.**
Organizations, as well as employees, are constantly changing. Perhaps a change in job responsibilities, coworkers, or surroundings within the organization would better suit the employee.

4. **Retrain the employee.**
The skill set of the employee may need to be upgraded or changed. Employees are typically much happier and better performers when they possess the skills they need to achieve a high level of success.

Stringent Measures

If, on the other hand, the employee is not salvageable, other actions will be necessary, such as:

1. Retrain supervisors in how to discipline problem employees.

Properly disciplining employees is one of the most difficult jobs of a supervisor. They should be trained on a regular basis about how to document ineffective performance, how to discuss performance problems with employees, and how to try to improve the situation. If all else fails, supervisors need to know how to terminate the problem employee.

2. Involve the human resource department.

Human resource professionals are skilled in how to discuss performance issues with employees. They are also knowledgeable about the relevant company rules and state and federal laws. Get them involved early in the improvement or termination process.

3. Start the paper trail now.

Supervisors should begin to document specific incidents of poor performance. These should be discussed with the employee as soon after the infraction as possible. The employee should also be told that this incident serves as a warning that they may be dismissed if improvements are not made within a specified time frame.

4. Senior management must promote the process.

Senior management must communicate to supervisors that it is important to the organization that they do their best to improve or terminate ineffective performers.

Conclusion

Employees hate it when they perceive that others are not pulling their own weight and management is doing nothing about it. Management needs to be proactive about solving the problem by identifying the root cause, changing the employee's job or supervisor, or retraining, disciplining, or terminating the employee. Contrary to management's fears, other employees in the organization will actually be pleased that management is taking appropriate action.

*Fifty percent of employees believe that the time they spend at
meetings is not time well spent.*

There are too many damn meetings.

A 200-person industry think tank had a long, proud history of providing cutting-edge research reports to its members. It was also
in total disarray. The presidency had changed hands several times
within just a few years, and the owners were looking for a buyer.

This was all very unsettling to the workforce. Key players were
constantly vying for power and influence. The managers and employees of the major departments had deep-seated mistrust for each other.
The organization had morphed into a group of separate silos unwilling
to cooperate with each other. Senior management was overcompensat-
ing by establishing interdepartmental meetings for just about everything. While the goal was to try to coordinate the activities of the
departments and maximize involvement, the meetings were typically
unproductive. They were characterized by lots of posturing, little commitment, and no real decision making or follow through.

Employees didn't really want to be at the meetings. They arrived
late, left early, and allowed themselves to be interrupted by keeping
their cell phones turned on. Some of the senior people even arranged
to have their secretaries interrupt the meeting and whisper into their
ear that they needed to leave to attend to an important phone call. They
weren't fooling anyone.

The meetings were chaotic. There was rarely an agenda. They often lasted for hours. Few said how they really felt. No decisions were ever really made. Instead of constructive discussions, everyone was just going through the motions. People returned to their offices shaking their heads and muttering under their breath, "What a waste of time."

No wonder our employee survey revealed that only 28 percent of employees believed that the time they spent at meetings was well spent. Even all ten members of the senior management team felt that way.

The Problem for Employers

Meetings serve many useful functions. They provide an opportunity for employees from different parts of the organization to communicate and cooperate with each other. They enable employees with different perspectives to provide input and help focus employees on organizational rather than just departmental or individual goals. Nevertheless, half of all employees believe the meetings they attend are a waste of time. Here are some reasons why:

1. *People arrive late.* When a meeting does not start on time, it is a waste of time for everyone. If six people attend a meeting and the start of that meeting is delayed for 10 minutes, that's a waste of one person-hour. Yet late attendance is more the rule than the exception. I often joke with the first person who attends one of my meetings by saying, "You're here on time, you must be new to the organization."

2. *Meetings take too long.* Many meetings have no clear pre-set agenda, objectives, or stopping time. They thus amble on endlessly with little purpose or direction.

3. *Too many people are invited.* Ever attend a meeting and ask yourself, "Why am I here?" Meeting leaders often over-invite because they don't want to offend anyone by leaving them off the list. But many of them would actually prefer not to be included.

4. *Meetings are very expensive.* Do the math. Let's say there is a meeting of ten people, each with salaries of $65,000. If you add in the cost of their benefits, they're each costing the company about $100,000 per year. Assuming they work forty hours per week, take three weeks of vacation, and have fifteen paid days off, they each make approximately $54 per hour. A two-hour meeting, therefore, costs the company $1,080, plus the cost of any food that is served. If more people attend or more senior folks are invited, the cost is even higher. This does not even take into account the lost productivity of each person who, instead of attending the meeting, could have been billing hours to clients or making products.

The Psychology of It All

Here are a few psychological reasons why employees find meetings to be a waste of time:

Not Enough Time Spent on Process

Content and *process* are the two major components of any meeting. Many psychologists would argue that 85 percent or more of any meeting should be devoted to process issues. Only then will the actual content (or work) of the committee run smoothly and quickly. Process refers to discussing how people feel "in the here and now" about the functioning of the group, the task at hand, how the decision will be made, and what role each person will play in the decision-making process.

Not Enough Diversity in Perspectives

Well-functioning groups need a combination of people who view the world in different ways. For example, some people are planners and doers. Others are more analytical. And still others do a great job looking into the future and seeing the big picture. The most productive and time-efficient meetings contain a combination of these different types of people.

Dissension Not Valued

One problem experienced by ineffective decision-making groups is a phenomenon that social psychologist Irving Janis called "group-think."[1] This happens when a powerful leader of a meeting makes it clear to the group what decision he wants to be made. The meeting then consists of everyone agreeing with the leader and not expressing any reservations or divergent views. This not only often leads to ineffective decisions, it's a waste of everyone's time.

Leadership Not Shared

Too often people are lazy and simply acquiesce to the person who called the meeting. They fail to share in the responsibility for the group's activities. When people are reluctant to participate and fail to become invested in the discussion, meetings are less efficient and people feel less committed to the outcome. The result is another waste of time. Leadership can take many forms, such as:

- Moving the group from one topic to another
- Summarizing the group's current thinking
- Expressing a feeling about the progress or lack of progress of the group
- Moving the group to consensus
- Objecting to a decision reached by the group

Lack of Commitment to the Meeting's Goals

If the group's members have different goals or don't care about the outcome, little good will result from the meeting. There will be no commitment to following through on the decisions of the group. The result again: a waste of time.

➲ Solutions

1. Put a time limit on meetings.

Tell people the meetings will start and end promptly. To get people to show up on time, make everyone late to the meeting pay into a special kitty that will be used for a holiday party.

When I worked for a large consulting firm, everyone's billable hours were very closely monitored. Lost time was lost money. They conducted an all-out war against wasted non-billable meeting time. They installed a high table with no chairs in a small conference room. The idea was to conduct short stand-up meetings with only a few participants. Also, the meeting room could only be reserved for a maximum of 30 minutes.

2. Use a process facilitator.

For a particularly important meeting, you might want to bring in a meeting facilitator, whose job it is to ensure that the meeting flows smoothly, that process issues are discussed, and that the objectives of the meeting are met. Or you might use as a facilitator someone from another part of the organization, or rotate the responsibility among group members.

3. Pay special attention to the end of the meeting.

Too often, people leave meetings before they have come to their natural conclusion. (Typically, they are running off to attend another nonproductive meeting.)

Ample time at the end of meetings should be devoted to two critical activities. First, discuss "next steps," including deciding who is responsible for doing what, and the deadline for each activity. And second, conduct a "good and welfare" discussion, where everyone is asked to say what they thought went well during the meeting, what did not, and what should be done at the next meeting to improve the process. People are also given the opportunity to express themselves about any topic of value to the group even if it is not on the agenda.

Conclusion

Employees resent management for wasting their time at unproductive meetings. The opportunity to interact with colleagues during meetings should make employees feel good, not frustrated. Meetings don't have to be a waste of time. To make them valuable, limit their length, be careful who you invite, focus on process, and pay particular attention to the end of the meeting.

Note

1.   I. Janis, *Groupthink* (Boston: Houghton Mifflin, 1972).

Part IV

Employees Feel Unappreciated

Sixty-one percent of employees are dissatisfied with their pay.

I'm not paid fairly.

During my senior year of high school I held a part-time job loading 50-pound sacks of fertilizer and garden supplies onto large trucks. We were paid by the hour, until the job was completed. There were three of us: my buddy, an elderly General Motors assembly worker, and me. I was anxious to impress, and worked hard and quickly my first evening. The second night, the GM worker cornered me and said sternly, "We work SLOWLY here, GET IT?" He didn't say that we did this to make more money, but that was obvious.

This behavior is not limited to physical laborers. A colleague of mine works in a management-consulting firm. Most of his clients are government agencies. They set what he considers a very low limit on how much his firm can charge per hour. He plays the game by saying that the project will take more hours than it actually does.

Several years ago I was consulting to a small utility in New England. Most of the unionized workforce had been with the organization for many years. Their biggest complaint was that the pay was too low. They told me, "We just go through the motions on Fridays, not doing any actual work because our paycheck only really covers us for four days."

The Problem for Employers

Many employees feel they are inadequately compensated for their work, believing they are paid unfairly compared to others performing similar work in other organizations. They therefore may feel justified in engaging in unethical behavior to compensate for what they perceive as low pay. This includes falsifying their time sheets and even stealing from their employer.

The truth is that most employees really have very little idea about how their compensation compares to other organizations. Work rules, benefits, time-off policies, and many other factors vary widely among organizations, making it difficult to compare apples to apples.

Employees assess the adequacy of their pay on many pieces of usually unreliable information. Some rely on what former coworkers tell them they are making at their new jobs. Whether the departed employees were truthful about their current compensation is unknown. Others cite the salary they saw listed in the newspaper for a similar job, but have no way of knowing if the job is really comparable or how the total compensation package compares to their current job. Even salary surveys are an inadequate method for employees to compare their pay to that in other organizations. The results will depend on which organizations chose to participate in the study, and they may not reflect the differences in cost of living or job responsibilities.

Although individual pay levels are kept secret in most organizations, many employees feel they are paid unfairly compared to others performing similar work in their own organization. In many cases, these perceptions of "internal pay inequity" are inaccurate. However, whether real or imagined, this can result in resentment and poor teamwork.

The Psychology of It All

Since pay levels are secret and employees rarely share this information, they base their views about internal inequity on two, often inaccurate, perceptions. First, in any work group there are usually one or two people who are viewed as poor performers. Employees assume that these employees are earning the same pay that they earn. This may not be true.

Second, most employees feel their own performance is above average. They therefore feel that if their pay is only average, that means they're being paid the same as less deserving employees. This too may not be true. Also, their perception about the superiority of their job performance may be inaccurate.

Pay is important to employees, of course, because it allows them to provide for themselves and their family, and they equate it with respect and recognition. It is an invisible badge they wear for the world to see, and for many, it has a major impact on their self-esteem.

Frederick Herzberg and his colleagues describe pay as a "hygiene factor"—as no more important than the office furniture, lights, and temperature. According to Herzberg, "hygienes" can't motivate or satisfy employees. They can only be a source of dissatisfaction.[1]

➲ Solutions

1. Clearly state your pay philosophy.

A pay philosophy is a simple statement about how the organization pays relative to the market. Stating such a philosophy makes it clear to employees and job applicants how they can expect to be paid. For example, a common pay philosophy might be, "We pay at or above the market level of pay in similar organizations in our area." The more specific the policy, the better, such as: "We pay at the 75th percentile for other mid-sized life insurance companies in downtown Boston, as reported in the annual ABC salary survey."

Some organizations make it clear to applicants and employees that they pay below the market. For example, nonprofit organizations are typically poor payers. Many employees are willing to live with the lower pay because they believe strongly in the mission of the organization.

Other organizations say they pay below the market but offer

other benefits instead. For example, one pharmaceutical research company pays below market rates for research scientists, but offers a family-friendly atmosphere. Leaving at 5:00 P.M. is accepted and encouraged. Taking time off to attend a child's soccer match during the workday is also accepted. The employees all knew when they accepted positions with the company that they were sacrificing pay for a better lifestyle.

2. Avoid paying by the hour.

I work with a computer professional to help me purchase equipment, install software, and solve problems that periodically occur. He used to charge me by the hour. When he helped me, it often seemed like we were focusing on time rather than results. I was looking at my watch, and he undoubtedly was looking at his. The faster he was able to solve my computer problems, the less money he made. It just didn't make sense to me. We changed our arrangement so that I now pay him a monthly retainer, which is much more satisfying for both of us.

Whenever possible, pay your employees for deliverables and results, not their time. Wouldn't it make sense to pay a salesperson who only works half-time as much as one who works full-time if they both achieved the same level of sales?

3. Use bonuses rather than pay increases.

Properly administered, bonuses can be much more motivating to employees than increases to their salary. They also are less expensive, because they don't commit the organization to pay the increased level of pay every year.

4. Train supervisors how to talk about pay.

It is important to convey the appropriate messages about pay to employees. Don't undermine your organization's compensation program by apologizing when you offer a pay increase that is not as high as the employee would like. Instead of expressing regret, talk about why they are being given a pay increase.

5. Weed out ineffective performers.

If poor performers earn the same as good performers, it signals to good performers that the quality of their work doesn't affect their pay.

Conclusion

Pay is important to employees, and many are unhappy about it. They hate management for not paying them more. But giving everyone a raise is usually not possible and would probably not solve the problem anyway. Instead, you can improve the way employees feel about their pay by better communicating a specific pay philosophy and demonstrating to them that their hard work will be rewarded.

Note

1. F. Herzberg et al., *Job Attitudes: Review of Research and Opinion* (Pittsburgh: Psychological Service of Pittsburgh, 1957).

Fifty-two percent of employees think they are paid unfairly compared with people in their organization who hold similar jobs.

It's just not right that we all receive the same pay.

One year I consulted to the behind-the-scenes operations group of a metropolitan airport. This 150-person group was in charge of security and maintenance of the airport facilities. The majority of the employees were unionized. Here are some of their complaints:

• *Equal Pay for Unequal Work.* A maintenance employee working on a team responsible for taking care of the grounds complained, "Although I've only been working here a short time, I work harder and do a much better job than anybody else here. But I am paid far less."

A member of the rescue squad agreed: "The people on our squad who have been working here the longest do the least amount of work, yet make the most money because of their seniority."

When I pointed out to them that this is actually the arrangement they had asked for and paid monthly dues to their union to negotiate for them, they just shrugged their shoulders and said it was still management's fault.

• *Pay Compression.* At another organization, one of the sales people on the floor complained, "I earn virtually the same as new employees, and I've been working here for three years." This is called "pay compression."

• *The Top-of-the-Range Blues.* I received an e-mail message from a storeowner who said, "I have forty employees who do mostly unskilled work. Many of them have been with us for more than ten years and have reached their maximum earning potential. My concern is that we have 'trapped' them in their jobs by treating them well, paying them decently for their type of work, and providing them with medical and dental insurance."

Most organizations have fixed pay grades that specify the amount of money that can be paid to employees in each position. The pay grades have a minimum and a maximum salary. Typically, new employees start at the bottom of the salary range and gradually move up as they receive pay increases.

The purpose of the pay grades is to make certain that the organization maintains good control over its total labor costs. The pay grades also help to maintain internal pay equity. For example, supervisors understandably become upset when their direct reports make more money than they do. But what should organizations do when their loyal, high performing employees reach the top of the pay grade? Typically, these employees continue to work with no pay increases except, perhaps, cost of living increases.

The problem is that these top-of-the-pay-grade employees may become frustrated and lose their motivation. They feel trapped.

The Problem for Employers

Employees want to believe that their good performance is recognized by management and appropriately compensated. Most don't want all employees to be paid an identical wage. Instead, they want the best performers to be paid the most. However, most also believe they are above average performers.

The problem is that when employees feel they are not paid what they deserve compared to others performing the same work in their organization, they become resentful. They resent the organization and their coworkers. They think, "That lazy SOB in the next office makes the same as I do. Why should I work harder when I'm not going to see it in my paycheck?" These thoughts are not good for employee morale or for maintaining a motivated workforce.

Although many organizations would very much like to pay employees performing the same work differently, it is often difficult to do so. Here's why:

1. *The Challenge of Objectively Measuring Performance.* It is difficult to measure the performance of many types of employees. Often, one must rely on the subjective ratings of supervisors. Their ratings may be biased or not comparable to those of other supervisors.

2. *Lack of Trust in Supervisory Ratings.* Employees don't trust supervisors to properly differentiate between good and poor performers. They therefore ask their union to negotiate across-the-board pay raises or raises based solely on tenure.

3. *Ease of Providing Equal Pay Increases to All.* Organizations find it much easier to pay everyone working the same job the same pay. They then don't have to worry about accurately measuring performance. They also believe that this will be easier to sell to employees. They can say, "Look, you're all part of the same team and we want to pay you the same since everyone needs to contribute equally to the team." But employees usually don't buy this logic, since it's obviously not true.

The Psychology of It All

Recall that equity theory predicts employees will most likely do one of five things when they believe they are receiving the same outcome (e.g., compensation) as those working at the same job but performing poorly. They can reduce their input (e.g., their job performance), increase their outcomes (e.g., by asking for a pay raise), increase the outcomes of others (e.g., rationalizing that those paid more really are performing better), reduce the outcome of others (e.g., try to reduce others' pay), or leave the situation. Reducing their own input is most likely.

➲ Solutions

1. Set clear expectations for applicants.

Be open and honest with job applicants about what will happen when they reach the top of their pay range. Tell them that when this eventually happens they will not be able to earn more in that position. Explain to them that while there are limits to the pay they can earn in the position, they will acquire valuable training and experience that will be useful to them in their career. This way employees will be able to join the organization with their eyes open.

2. Offer additional responsibilities to top-of-the-range employees.

For example, assign them the job of training new employees, or ask them to work on special projects. If you've given them greater responsibilities, you can feel justified in offering them more money.

3. Widen pay ranges.

The "pay compression" problem is common in organizations. In order to attract employees to join the organization, publicly advertised starting pay rates are relatively high. This annoys incumbents because they see that new employees are earning the same or almost the same as they are earning. Expanding the salary ranges can help.

4. Avoid paying by the hour.

Paying by the hour makes little sense for many jobs because employees develop ingenious and often unethical approaches to stretching their work into the full eight hours, even when it can be accomplished in far less time.

Also, if paid by the hour, the faster employees work, the less money they will make for the work they perform. If you pay by the hour, you will be paying primarily for attendance and will not be able to compensate people differentially based on their performance.

5. Don't stop trying to tie pay to performance.
It is simply too easy to give up on the task of properly measuring the performance of employees. Continually refine how you evaluate their performance and train supervisors how to use the performance review process.

6. Offer longevity bonuses.
Provide selected top-of-the-range employees with bonuses twice a year (e.g., December and June). This is not a raise and therefore would not increase the cost of employee benefits, such as company contributions to the 401(k) plan.

7. Promote your best performers.
If possible, provide real promotions to your best performers, not just changes in job titles. Offer an increase in salary commensurate with their new responsibilities.

8. Encourage those unhappy with their pay to leave.
No one benefits from unhappy employees. It might be best for both the organization and the employees if you encourage those who are unhappy with their pay and not worthy of promotion to leave. Tell them that because of their organizational knowledge and loyalty you would hate to see them go, but there is a limit to the flexibility of the pay system. Offer to provide them with excellent references.

Conclusion

Employees want to feel that they will be paid more than those coworkers who are contributing less to the organization. They resent management if they are not. Do your best to pay for performance. Set clear expectations about pay to new employees, widen pay ranges, avoid paying by the hour, offer longevity bonuses, and either promote those who are frustrated that they have reached the top of the pay scale, or encourage them to leave the organization.

Fifty-four percent of employees say their performance reviews are useless.

My performance reviews are useless.

A high-tech manufacturer outside of Boston had been spun off of a much larger company and was now privately held. Within the first three months more than one-third of the workforce was laid off. Needless to say, the survivors were extremely unhappy and feared for their jobs. We conducted an employee survey and found that employees were dissatisfied with just about everything (i.e., management, their supervisors, communication, teamwork, their pay, and their performance reviews).

I advised management to begin with tangible and visible changes that would affect all employees. One of my recommendations was to make sure all employees received their performance reviews on a timely basis. The president agreed to make this a number one priority, one that he would adhere to as well.

In a follow-up survey six months later, the results had improved dramatically. When the president was asked what they had done differently, he said, "The only real change we implemented was to conduct those damn performance reviews on time." Surprisingly, that one major change had a strong impact on how employees felt about their supervisors, management, pay, communications, and a host of other issues.

The Problem for Employers

Performance reviews are extremely important to employees, but they have severe reservations about how they are conducted. Here are some of the complaints that I hear most often:

- "My supervisor is never around and has no idea of what I do on my job. How on earth can he evaluate me?"

- "My supervisor just takes the easy way out. She says nice things about me during the review and then recommends that I receive the same raise as everyone else."

- "My performance reviews are always late."

- "My supervisor is biased. He doesn't like me even though I am a very good performer."

- "The rating instrument makes no sense. I don't understand it and my supervisor doesn't understand it either. Everyone in the company is rated using the same form, which is totally unrelated to my job functions."

- "The only performance feedback I receive all year is during my annual review. If I am doing something wrong, why does she wait the whole year to tell me about it?"

- "My supervisor never comes up with useful suggestions."

- "I disagreed with my supervisor's evaluation and refused to sign it."

- "Performance reviews are a waste of time."

Even high performers have concerns about the usefulness of their performance reviews. Everyone can improve his job performance, yet those who receive glowing reviews from their supervisors are usually provided with little guidance about how they can become even better at their jobs.

Most employees feel they are above-average performers. This, of course, is mathematically impossible, which means many employees receive information about their job performance that is inconsistent with their own beliefs.

One reason many employees find it difficult to receive negative feedback about their job performance and then bounce back and improve is that they deny rather than accept negative feedback. They deny the feedback because it is just too strong of an affront to their personal self-image. Another reason is that it is very difficult for them to change. If you have been performing your job the same way for a long period of time, the probability of your being able to make radical changes is low.

Although most employees might disagree, many really do need constructive feedback to help them improve their job performance. If employees don't continually improve, the organization won't either.

The Psychology of It All

The annual performance review is one of the most difficult tasks for any supervisor. Supervisors must not only evaluate the performance of their subordinates, they must feed back the information to them in a way that is constructive and useful. Few supervisors are able to do this well. Is it any wonder many supervisors avoid conducting them?

One of the reasons supervisors find performance reviews difficult is that they desperately want to avoid conflict. They fear that their employees will disagree, debate, and fight their evaluations. They therefore take the easy road and provide feedback that is generally positive, avoiding areas in need of improvement. As a result, the performance review is not very useful to the employee or the organization.

Another reason performance reviews are difficult for supervisors is that they have trouble distinguishing between different levels of performance. What an average performer needs to do to become a superior performer is unclear to them. They therefore find it difficult to tell employees what they need to do to improve.

Conceptually, supervisors are the "middles" in the organizational hierarchy. Their job is to get the "lowers" (i.e., their direct reports) on board to perform the work demanded by the "uppers." The strategy many supervisors use to successfully influence their direct reports is to befriend them, to pitch in themselves to do the work, and to be viewed as more of a lower than an upper (i.e., one of the boys). But evaluating employees is inconsistent with this relationship strategy. Supervisors find it difficult to evaluate their "friends." They fear that acting more like uppers than lowers will make it difficult for them to maintain the cooperation of lowers.

Supervisors also fear that an unfavorable performance review may lead an employee to decrease her job performance. This could happen because she becomes so angry or upset that she is unable to perform well. Or she could intentionally reduce her performance to get back at the supervisor. Sometimes a perfectly cooperative and compliant employee may turn passive-aggressive following a negative performance review.

Many supervisors are consequently reluctant to accept the responsibility of judging their direct reports. They don't like being evaluated themselves, and they do not want to evaluate others. They don't want to be in the position of providing judgments that will affect the financial and psychological well-being of a coworker.

➲ Solutions

1. Provide continuous feedback.

Supervisors should get in the habit of providing performance feedback to their employees on a regular basis. This makes the performance review much easier for both the supervisor and the employee. For the supervisor, the meeting is then just a review or summary of the feedback that has been provided throughout the year. For employees, the review will contain no surprises.

2. Adopt a developmental mindset.

Supervisors can avoid much of the pain of the performance review process by viewing it as a developmental rather than an evaluative exercise. Their job is to provide honest feedback, advice, and counsel to help employees improve their job performance. Instead of a meeting to discuss a report card, the review should be more of a counseling session.

3. Skip the money part.

Salary and bonuses, of course, are very important to employees, but they also want constructive feedback. Salary decisions are influenced by many factors outside the control of the supervisor or the employee. Discussions about money should be held separately, apart from the performance review.

4. Involve employees in setting goals.

Employees will be much more committed to improving their job performance if they have a hand in setting goals. The goals should be specific, measurable, acceptable to both employee and supervisor, realistic, and contain a clear time frame.

5. Focus on behaviors, not traits.

Feedback should be a discussion of specifically observed behavior rather than an evaluation of an employee's personality. This applies to both positive and negative behaviors. For example, it is much more effective to say, "You did a great job proofreading that report yesterday and catching those typos" than to say, "You have very good attention to detail."

6. Conduct performance discussions, not lectures.

Employees should be involved in setting their own performance goals and articulating plans for their own professional development. Supervisors should talk about the behavior they have observed, but also ask employees for their views of areas where improvements can be made. By involving employees in their own development, they will be more likely to take positive action.

7. Conduct annual performance reviews on time.

Late performance reviews are a slap in the face to employees. Delaying the performance review is a signal that the supervisors do not care about the employee's development. Reviews should be conducted on time.

8. Train supervisors.

All supervisors need to be trained on a regular basis about how to provide effective performance feedback. It is an important skill that must be continually refined.

Conclusion

Many employees find little value in the performance reviews they receive and resent management for not being able to provide them with useful feedback. To make these reviews more useful, supervisors should provide continuous feedback throughout the year and view the performance review as more of a developmental than evaluative exercise. Organizations should do a better job of providing training in how to conduct performance reviews, and most importantly, make sure they are conducted at the scheduled time.

②③

*Seven out of ten employees say there is no link between their
pay and their job performance.*

There's no link between my pay and my job performance.

H ere's yet another tale of woe in my sister Andrea's tumultuous
employment history.

Andrea was placed on 60-day probation as a collections specialist
for a medical equipment rental company because she had a low "collection ratio." They calculated this ratio by monitoring the percentage
of the outstanding balances assigned to her to collect each month. She
was actually doing a good job of collecting, but her ratio didn't reflect
it. That's because any account with a balance of $5,000 or more was
assigned to her supervisor, who was doing a poor job of collecting. But
the company had no way to separate Andrea's collection ratio from
that of her supervisor's. The result was that my sister's ratio was mis-
leadingly low.

When she brought this to the attention of management she was
told, "There is nothing we can do. It would be extremely difficult to
untangle it all. We're all a team here. Aren't you a team player?"

Determined to keep her job, Andrea politely offered to help her
supervisor collect the larger balances. The supervisor (who, by the way
was not on 60-day probation) declined her offer. Andrea was let go
after the 60 days. Does this make sense to you? It doesn't to me.

I frequently hear employees say, "We all make the same money in this department but some of us really earn it and others don't. It's just not fair." Some comment that the company has no effective way to measure how well they are really performing. Others say, "It doesn't matter how well you perform here, you'll never see it in your paycheck." Still others comment, "My supervisor has no guts. He takes the simple way out and gives everyone the same pay increases each year."

The Problem for Employers

Employees in both manufacturing and service organizations consistently say that a strong link between their pay and their job performance is very important to them. They want to feel their good work is appreciated and that they are appropriately compensated, but most organizations do a poor job of tying pay to job performance. Many employees, therefore, feel that no matter how hard they work it will have little or no impact on their pay.

One problem is that even when organizations are committed to tying pay to job performance, they often have a difficult time differentiating between good and superior performers. For many jobs, individual performance cannot be measured objectively. Therefore, the organization must rely on subjective ratings by supervisors, and many supervisors are just not up to the task. Also, supervisors in different parts of the organization may have very different views of average and superior performance.

Some organizations try unsuccessfully to combat the problem by using profit-sharing programs that link the pay of all employees to the success of the organization. If the company makes a profit, a portion of that money is shared with all employees. But most employees don't buy into this profit-sharing approach. They see very little real connection between the quality of their performance and the profits of the organization. Also, profit shares are usually distributed equally to all employees with no differentiation among different levels of performance. Employees, therefore, continue to feel that their superior performance is not being recognized.

Most organizations throw up their hands at the problem and just offer across-the-board annual pay increases. Others tell their employees that they pay for performance, even when they really don't. These solutions make nobody happy and only exacerbate the problem.

Organizations that attempt to tie pay to job performance face three major challenges:

1. Concern About Alienating Good Performers

Organizations worry that if they provide pay increases for some and not others, they will undoubtedly offend or alienate some good employees who may even decide to leave.

2. Necessity of Relying on Subjective Measurements

Without readily available objective measures to differentiate between good and poor job performance, supervisory performance ratings are plagued by a host of problems, including:

• *Halo.* The tendency for raters to develop a general, overall impression of the employee and base their ratings on that impression rather than the employee's actual job performance.

• *Bias.* Ratings can be influenced by the supervisor's conscious or unconscious bias toward employees of a certain gender, race, ethnic origin, or sexual preference.

• *Leniency.* The tendency for supervisors to rate all their employees as superior.

• *Personal Equations.* This refers to the fact that supervisors vary in how they use the rating scales. If you happen to work for a supervisor who rarely provides high ratings, you will never see a good pay raise, whereas those working for supervisors who are more lenient with their ratings will always see good pay increases.

• *Forced Distribution Problems.* One commonly used approach to avoid the problems of leniency and halo is to force supervisors to dis-

tribute their ratings. For example, a supervisor with ten direct reports
might be required to limit her most superior and harshest ratings to
only two employees each. The problem is that some supervisors may
really have more than two superior performers, while others may have
none.

3. Difficulty of Using Objective Measures

Organizations that attempt to use objective measures instead of supervisory ratings face other problems:

• *Opportunity Bias.* A salesperson complains that the way her
sales success is measured should take into account the fact that her
sales territory is much smaller than the territories of other salesmen
in the company and she, therefore, has less of an opportunity to be
successful.

• *Criterion Contamination.* A claims adjuster for an auto insurance company argues that the large volume of expensive claims he
processed for the company was not his fault. It was due to events out
of his control (i.e., the snowy weather during the previous winter led
to an unusually high number of accidents for his policyholders).

• *Deficiency.* The performance of sales personnel at a consumer
electronics store is calculated from the ratings they receive from customer satisfaction surveys. The problem is that the surveys are mailed
to the customers' homes after they make a purchase, and not all of
them complete and return them. The sales personnel feel that those
who are satisfied generally don't bother to fill them out.

• *Irrelevancy.* The performance of junior consultants is typically
based on the number of billable hours they assign to clients. However,
they have no sales responsibilities and are totally dependent on others
to bring in the work that they then conduct. Their billable hours may
be low because others aren't doing a good job of selling, not because
they aren't trying to do as much work as possible.

- *Group Rather than Individual Measures.* Many organizations make judgments about individual performance based on the group's performance. For example, you might be the star employee in your department, but if the department is not meeting its goals, your individual performance rating will suffer.

- *Dishonesty.* Many organizations now use a 360-degree feedback approach to measure performance. In addition to supervisors, employees' direct reports and peers are also asked to rate their performance. For their own selfish reasons, these raters may be less than honest. For example, direct reports might fear retribution from their supervisors, and peers might worry about damaging fragile collegial relationships or that they will receive low ratings when the tables are turned and it is their turn to be rated.

The problem is that when employees see little connection between their job performance and their pay, their motivation will likely decline.

The Psychology of It All

Expectancy theory, conceived by renowned psychologist Victor Vroom, tells us that employee work motivation is dependent upon three factors. The first is called the *effort-performance expectancy* ($E \rightarrow P$). Those with high $E \rightarrow P$ expectancies believe that if they work hard they definitely will achieve a high level of performance. Those with low $E \rightarrow P$ expectations believe that even if they work hard, they will not be able to achieve a high level of performance.[1]

The second factor is called the *performance-outcome expectancy* ($P \rightarrow O$). This is the expectation employees have that if they perform well they will achieve outcomes they desire, such as a pay raise, bonus, or promotion. Those with high $P \rightarrow O$ expectations believe there is a strong link between achieving a high level of performance and receiving the outcomes they value. Those with low $P \rightarrow O$ expectations do not believe this to be true.

The third factor is called *valence* (V). This is the value people attach to potential outcomes they might receive. Some employees place a higher value than others on certain outcomes, such as pay raises and promotions.

The equation that combines these three factors is:

$$\text{Work motivation} = \Sigma \ (E \rightarrow P) \ (P \rightarrow O) \ (V)$$

Thus, according to expectancy theory, employee motivation is equal to the sum of one's E→P expectations times one's P→O expectations times one's valences. What this means is that if there is a perceived weak link between pay and job performance, the performance-outcome expectancy lowers the employee's motivation.

➲ Solutions

Here are a few suggestions that can help.

1. **Make your pay-for-performance philosophy clear to employees.** There are plenty of good reasons why you might NOT want to link pay to performance. For example:

- There are no major differences in how well employees perform their jobs.
- It is too difficult to measure differences in job performance.
- There is not enough money available to make a big enough difference in how average and above-average performers are paid.
- Linking pay and performance is inconsistent with management's philosophy.

However, employees typically assume that above-average performers will receive higher pay increases than average performers.

At the very least, management needs to be upfront with employees about whether they intend to try to link pay to performance.

2. Rate supervisors on how well they rate their subordinates.

Supervisors often sabotage the organization's efforts to improve the pay of good performers by giving everyone in their work group high ratings. Management needs to analyze the ratings of supervisors and base supervisors' pay, in part, on the quality of the ratings they give to their workers.

3. Train supervisors how to talk about pay.

Many supervisors undermine their organization's pay for performance efforts by saying things like, "I wish we could pay you more, but all we can do is increase your salary by 5 percent." Instead, they should be saying, "I am delighted to tell you that due to your excellent performance this past year, we are increasing your salary 5 percent." Supervisors need to be taught how to appropriately communicate to employees that their good performance is being rewarded.

4. Use objective performance measures.

Many jobs tie pay to the subjective ratings of supervisors. These ratings are often contaminated by a host of factors, including personal bias, halo, favoritism, central tendency, and leniency. Every attempt should be made to base pay decisions on objective criteria such as sales, attendance, complaints, quality, and productivity.

Be creative. Just because objective measures haven't been used before, doesn't mean they can't be introduced now. For many jobs, useful metrics can be created for a variety of performance indices such as sales, speed, errors, cost control, efficiency, customer complaints, internal and external customer satisfaction, quality, and quantity of production. Make sure these measures are appropriate for the job and contain no obvious sources of contamination, bias, deficiency, or irrelevancy.

5. Be cautious when using 360-degree feedback.
Receiving feedback from peers, subordinates, and others can be a valuable developmental exercise for employees. However, basing personnel decisions such as pay, promotions, probation, and termination on this feedback is problematic. The motivation of peers and subordinates is not the same as that of an immediate supervisor who is accountable to the organization for providing an accurate performance rating.

6. Use multiple measures.
It is rare that one type of performance measure, such as an individual's sales figures or supervisory rating, provides an accurate assessment of total performance. A variety of different types of measures should be used.

Conclusion

Employees typically want to be paid commensurate with the quality of their job performance. Doing so requires a commitment to a carefully constructed pay-for-performance program using relevant measures, all of which are clearly communicated to employees.

Note

1.   V. H. Vroom, *Work and Motivation* (New York: Wiley, 1964).

The cost of my benefits is eating up my paycheck.

M y wife received a 5 percent raise last year, but she also received an increase in the amount of money deducted from her paycheck for health insurance. The net result: a decrease in her take-home pay. This is a common frustration for U.S. workers.

The Problem for Employers

The cost of health care, which has risen astronomically in the past few decades, is crippling many companies. When General Motors recently reported a $1.1 billion first-quarter loss, it announced that the increased costs of providing health-care coverage for its employees, retirees, and their dependents was the most significant factor. The company reported that health-care expenditures amounted to $1,525 per car produced, and that there is more health care than steel in a GM vehicle's price tag.

Organizations have responded to the sharp increase in the cost of benefits, especially health insurance, by:

- Switching to managed care programs
- Shifting more of the premium expense to employees
- Forcing employees to pay more for their health insurance by raising deductible and co-payment levels

- Cutting back on the services that the health insurance covers

- Increasing the eligibility requirements (e.g., increasing the waiting period for coverage of new employees)

- Offering health insurance to employees but not to their families

An increasingly large number of organizations are refusing to offer health insurance to their workers altogether. Millions of employees are outraged. They feel that:

- They are entitled to health insurance from their employer.

- They and their families should be fully covered.

- Their employer should absorb most, if not all, of the cost increases.

The Psychology of It All

Employees have come to expect that they will receive health-care benefits from their employer. They view it as an entitlement. Frederick Herzberg would call this benefit "a hygiene factor," just like pay and the physical working conditions. As such, it cannot satisfy employees or motivate them. Its absence or reduction can, however, lead to dissatisfaction and decreased motivation. Despite the fact that employees know the cost of health insurance has risen dramatically, they view any increase in their cost or any decline in services as a take-away.

⊃ Solutions

1. Re-evaluate your current health insurer.
Conduct an extensive evaluation of the company's current offerings to make sure you have the best coverage available in the area at the best cost.

2. Switch to a single carrier.
Switching from multiple carriers to a single carrier eliminates choices for employees, but in the short term it can help employers negotiate more favorable rates.

3. Tell employees what they actually receive for their premium dollars.
A few years ago I spent ten days in the hospital for a heart problem. I received excellent care in a cardiac intensive care unit, was seen by many leading medical experts, and received dozens of expensive procedures. I never saw a bill and really have no idea of the total cost of my stay, but I would guess that it ran into the hundreds of thousands of dollars. If employees knew the actual cost of health care, it might soften the pain of seeing their large monthly payroll deductions for medical premiums.

4. Communicate how much the organization is paying for cost increases.
Many organizations do a poor job of communicating information about health insurance cost increases. If employees are going to be partners in paying for their benefits, they should be kept well informed about the coverage, the negotiations with the insurer, cost increases, and the percentage of the increase that the employer is planning to pass on to employees.

5. Produce total compensation statements.
Organizations rarely receive any credit from employees for shouldering the bulk of the cost of employee benefits. This is due, in part, to a lack of communication. Annual *total compensation statements* can help employees gain a better understanding of the actual cost of their salaries, bonuses, and benefits.

6. Increase deductibles and co-payments rather than premiums.
Increasing the deductible and co-payment levels can help save money by making employees more accountable for their medical

expenditures. Many people would prefer this type of cost increase to an increase in their monthly contributions.

7. Provide choices.
Health plan products can be creatively designed to provide a range of options that can match a person's budget and family circumstances. Provide a broad range of options, such as the number of doctors available in the plan and the amount of co-payments and deductibles.

8. Establish flexible medical spending accounts.
These accounts allow an employee to purchase qualified benefits, including medical and dental expenses, using pretax dollars. At the beginning of each year, employees designate how much they want to contribute to the account.

9. Promote wellness.
Employers who promote positive behavioral changes—such as smoking cessation, weekly exercise, and moderation of alcohol consumption—can decrease their long-term medical plan costs. These savings can be passed on to employees.

10. Help make employees better health-care consumers.
Employers can also help reduce their health-care costs by making their employers better consumers. If they have a better understanding of medicine, they might not need to visit the doctor as often. They might also learn when it is and is not necessary to make an expensive emergency room visit.

Conclusion

Employers will need to use a variety of creative approaches to reduce the costs of benefits and reduce the pain felt by many employees. In order to avoid shouldering the blame for these increases, management should re-evaluate their health insurers, provide choices, communicate better with employees about the cost of health care, and promote wellness.

2 5

Fifty-eight percent of employees say there are few advancement opportunities in their organization.

It's impossible to get promoted here.

The junior faculty of a small liberal arts college tucked away in a remote rural town in northern New England was in an uproar. Only 14 percent felt there were advancement opportunities at the college, and only 13 percent felt that the most competent faculty members were being promoted. No junior faculty member had received tenure for the past ten years. The college already had a large number of tenured faculty members, who were all planning on staying with the college for many more years until they retired. That left little room for advancement for others.

The Problem for Employers

Good employees want to be promoted. Promotions mean more money, more prestige, and greater responsibility. If too much time goes by without a promotion, they will be unhappy and may leave. Here are six reasons organizations are having a difficult time offering advancement opportunities:

1. More companies are contracting out rather than expanding, which leads to fewer opportunities for advancement.

2. Mergers and acquisitions often lead to downsizing instead of promotions.

3. A new kind of glass ceiling is emerging. The large crop of baby boomers who have reached management positions are staying at their jobs longer and are making it difficult for talented younger employees to move up.

4. Organizations are becoming flatter, limiting the number of supervisory and management positions available.

5. Promoting employees requires paying them more. This puts a strain on the budgets of many organizations.

6. College graduates join organizations with unrealistic expectations about their advancement potential.

The Psychology of It All

Psychologists Richard Steers of the University of Oregon and Lyman Porter of the University of California at Irvine theorize that two factors influence whether employees will seriously consider leaving their organization if their rate of promotion is slow: their expectations of promotion, and their self-perceived level of contribution.[1]

Employees have different expectations about being promoted. Some enter the organization with very high expectations. This can be due to a number of factors, including their promotion history in other organizations, their success in school, their desire for a certain standard of living, or the expectations of their parents, friends, or spouses. Those who have higher expectations are more likely to be disappointed when their rate of promotion does not match their desires.

Employees also vary in how they perceive their own contributions to the organization. Two employees with the same skill level, job accomplishments, and performance ratings can have radically different self-appraisals of their worth to the organization. Those with higher self-appraisals will be more disappointed by a slow rate of promotion.

➲ Solutions

1. Set realistic expectations for employees.

Psychologist John Wanous conducted research on the effects of realistic versus unrealistic job previews during the interviewing of new employees. He found that employees who are told exactly what to expect, both positive and negative, are eventually more satisfied on the job and less likely to leave than those who receive unrealistic job previews. He hypothesized that a realistic explanation of the job helps individuals make better decisions about the match between their expectations and what the job will be able to provide.[2] Another psychologist, W. J. McGuire, theorized that realistic job previews serve as a "vaccination" for new employees.[3] This dosage of the truth helps employees better deal with the organizational reality they will eventually face.

Prior to offering positions to new employees, tell them in a straightforward manner how likely or unlikely they are to be promoted within one, three, and five years. Also, be brutally honest about promotion possibilities during employee performance reviews and developmental discussions.

2. Be sure to point out opportunities for improvement.

If a supervisor says to an employee, "Your job performance is excellent and there is really nothing I can suggest for you to improve," the employee could easily believe that she is a strong candidate for promotion. If there are no positions available, she could be disappointed. Job performance can always be improved, even for the best employees. Point this out.

3. Promote the best.

Our research shows that three out of five employees believe their company does not promote the most competent employees. Needless to say, when employees feel that the wrong people are being promoted, they will be unhappy and resentful. Be sure to promote only the most competent people.

4. Create new positions.

In some organizations, it is possible to offer "mini" rather than "full" promotions, such as junior programmer to senior programmer, credit specialist I to credit specialist II, or production worker to team leader. But be careful not to just change the name of the person's job. Also increase their job responsibilities and pay.

5. Offer technical track promotions.

In many organizations, the only way strong technical employees, such as engineers and programmers, can advance is to accept a promotion to supervisor or manager. The problem is that they may not have the skills needed to succeed as managers. Create a technical career ladder so that you can give these employees more responsibilities and more pay without forcing them to become supervisors.

6. Promote from within.

Employees become unhappy when they see their organizations hire new employees into positions they feel they could have handled if they had been promoted and given a chance. Adopting a consistent policy of promoting from within, whenever possible, can increase employee commitment.

7. Move people around.

Consider moving promising employees you are unable to promote into different jobs where they may have more potential for advancement.

Conclusion

Keeping your best performers is obviously important. Although many of them may be deserving of a promotion, advancement opportunities are often limited. Organizations should set realistic expectations for new employees, be sure to promote only the most competent, and be creative in how to promote employees and provide them with added responsibilities.

Notes

1. S. M. Steers and L. W. Porter, *Motivation and Work Behavior* (New York: McGraw-Hill, 1975).

2. J. P. Wanous, *Organizational Entry: Recruitment, Selection, and Socialization of Newcomers* (Reading, Mass: Addison-Wesley, 1980).

3. W. J. McGuire, "Inducing resistance to persuasion." In L. Berkowitz (ed.), *Advances in Experimental Social Psychology*, Volume III (New York: Academic Press, 1964).

Part V

W-O-R-K Should Be More Than a Four-Letter Word

I hate coming to work. It's become just a job for me now.

Nothing disturbs me more than when I hear someone talking about his work and saying, "It's just a job." No one should be unhappy with his work.

What people do for a living has always fascinated me. Wherever I go, I ask people what they like about their work and what they dislike. (My wife gets upset when I ask this at purely social occasions.) But I'm interested on both a personal and professional level. I love what I do for a living and am happy when someone asks me about it.

But to my surprise and chagrin, many people don't like to talk about what they do for a living. For some, this is because they would rather talk about their kids, their hobbies, or politics. But for most, it's because they really don't enjoy their work. To them, it's "just a job," and they would rather not think about it once they're away from it. How sad.

One night I attended a holiday dinner at a good friend's house. There were several of his family's relatives and friends whom I had never met. True to form, I asked each of them what they did for a living. One person told me he was a computer network professional for a well-known retail chain. I asked him what he liked about his job.

He said, "Well, it's a job." When I probed further it was clear he really didn't want to elaborate. He repeated, "It's just a job."

Many people are unhappy with their work. For some, it is because of the organization they work for or their supervisor, but for many it is because of the actual work they perform. They have been doing it for many years and are simply burnt out. The work has lost its meaning for them and they just don't enjoy it anymore.

I've had the opportunity to conduct many outplacement workshops where I help people who have recently lost their jobs try to figure out what they want to do next. I begin the workshop by going around the room and asking each person to say what ideas they have. Typically, about half of the people say they just don't know, but that they do know they want to do something different. Many talk about finding a totally different kind of job or turning their hobby into a profitable business. They are worried, however, that they have little experience in a new field and might have to take a pay cut. I tell them that if that's what they really want to do, they owe it to themselves and their family to do it. Do what you love, follow your passion, and the money will eventually follow.

Here are a few examples of people I know who successfully made the transition. There is a man in his mid-60s in our town who had spent his entire career as a manufacturing supervisor. He worked at a number of companies and was usually forced to find a new job when the companies moved or went under. He had had it. What he really wanted to do was start a fix-it business. He loved using his hands and doing small projects around the house. He found out quickly that there were a great many people in need of his services, including me. He followed his passion and has never been happier.

I also know a computer whiz who was working as a Mac programmer for a software development company. When he was laid off, instead of pursuing another highly technical programming job, he took stock of himself and realized that what he really liked best about the work he had performed in all of his jobs was teaching others how to use their computers. He started a business that helps individuals and small businesses purchase their computers, install software, and use basic programs like word processors and spreadsheets. He loves what he does, and his new company has flourished.

The Problem for Employers

Unhappy employees are unproductive and drain the energy of others. That's just common sense, and management should not ignore the problem.

One of the reasons people do enjoy the work they perform is because they self-select themselves throughout their career. They attend schools where they can learn things of interest to them, and they choose jobs where they can use their valued skills and abilities. For example, those who are more analytical-minded choose to become engineers, computer professionals, scientists, or service technicians. They wouldn't think of working as a social worker or a human resource professional.

But there are also many who just end up working at a particular job or in a type of organization without ever really thinking about whether it's a good fit. For example, in outplacement workshops for members of the banking industry I ask the group, "How many of you grew up saying to yourself, 'What I really want to do is be a banker'"? Not one person has ever raised a hand. Most ended up as bankers because they needed a job at the time, a friend was working there, or they responded to a newspaper ad—in other words, out of convenience. Also out of convenience, they remained bankers. Eventually, they grew to view their work unhappily as "just a job."

This is a problem not only for organizations. For employees, not enjoying one's job reduces their enthusiasm and the quality of their lives.

The Psychology of It All

Different types of people have very different concepts of what work means to them. For some, work is purely a means to an end. They are interested in making as much money as possible as fast as they can. For others, work means helping people. These people are attracted to professions like social work, psychology, and health care. For still others, work means using their creativity. They may be attracted to professions such as architecture or the arts. For others, working for a cause they truly believe in is important. They may choose to work for a nonprofit organization. I happen to be among those for whom independence—working for myself—is the most important single work criterion.

The common denominator for all of these people who enjoy their work is that their work:

- Fully uses their skills and abilities.
- Challenges them.
- Allows them to grow.
- Enables them to feel successful.

Those who say their work is just a job are missing out on one or more of these intrinsic rewards.

❑ Solutions

1. Help employees see the light.
Employees who are just going through the motions and who don't have their heart in their work are doing a disservice to both themselves and their employer. They should be encouraged to learn more about what they really want to do either in their current organization or even in a different one. Employee training programs can help them better understand the possibilities.

2. Enrich jobs.
Find ways to introduce more of what Herzberg calls "motivators." Providing employees with more challenges, growth opportunities, and responsibilities can be rejuvenating.

3. Provide other opportunities.

Some employees can be "saved" if you transfer them to other parts of the organization and train them to take on different jobs.

4. Let your people go.

If employees are unhappy with their actual work and you are not able to provide them with alternatives, encourage them to leave. Do so in a positive way. Level with them. Tell them that you can see they are unhappy. Explain to them that although they have been excellent employees and are perfectly welcome to stay, for their own good it is probably time for them to move on with their career and explore other alternatives.

Conclusion

"It's just a job" is an unacceptable attitude. No one should settle for an unrewarding job, and it makes good business sense for organizations to do everything possible to rekindle the enthusiasm of employees.

There's no job security here.

B usiness headlines regularly report news of billion-dollar acquisitions, followed by massive layoffs. At the same time the CEOs receive record salaries and millions of dollars in "golden parachutes."

During the recession of 1993 I was working for a 71-office international consulting firm at plush offices in Wellesley Hills, Massachusetts. I had been a hard-working, loyal employee for four years. My job was to market, sell, and conduct employee opinion surveys for companies in New England.

But the economy was failing. Layoffs were rampant. Organizations in New England were pulling back on employee opinion surveys and certainly weren't asking high-priced consulting firms to help them. I was also losing my allies in the firm. My best friend in the company, who had recruited me, saw the writing on the wall and transferred to greener pastures in one of the company's west coast offices. His boss, another one of my key supporters, left for a job in the main headquarters.

As my sales and billable hours continued to slide, I knew my days were numbered. I felt paralyzed and scared. None of my intensive marketing efforts were yielding new business. There was nobody I could talk to in the office or who cared to help me. I came to work each day with a gnawing feeling in my stomach. I had difficultly sleeping and gained 15 pounds.

One memorable afternoon, my boss asked me, "Do you have a minute?" I knew that my time had come. He told me, "Bruce, people aren't buying what you're selling. We are going to have to lay you off." Even though I knew it was coming, I was devastated.

It certainly didn't feel that way at the time, but looking back, this was the single best thing that had ever happened to me in my personal life.

The Problem for Employers

Employees are pawns in the cruel corporate chess game of layoffs, mergers, acquisitions, and restructuring. Here is how they fight back, and how the negative consequences of their actions affect their employers:

1. *Carrying Multiple Jobs.* Employees realize that they can't put all of their eggs in one basket, so they take on second jobs or freelancing jobs. The result is that employers no longer receive the undivided focus of their employees.

2. *Demanding Portable Benefits.* Employees are no longer content with pensions that require them to stay with the same company for many years. They know that their tenure with their current company may be temporary and that the duration of their employment is out of their control. Employees would much prefer matching 401(k) plans that they can carry with them when they leave an organization. Expensive defined benefit retirement programs no longer guarantee long-term employee commitment.

3. *Withdrawing Psychologically.* Many employees will remain aloof to your cries for teamwork and commitment to organizational goals. Instead, they have developed a "what's-in-it-for-me" (WIIFM) attitude. Traditional motivators, such as climbing the corporate ladder and becoming known as a good team player, are not as effective as they once were.

4. *Adopting an Adversarial Relationship.* Employees have become cynical and no longer trust senior management like they once did. Their loyalty and commitment to their workplace have become fragile, and their priorities are seemingly at odds with organizational goals.

5. *Constantly Planning Escape Routes.* It is very difficult to motivate employees who would prefer to be somewhere else. Employees upgrade their skills not to help their current employer, but to help themselves land their next job. Other employees will be constantly scheming to take away clients and start their own businesses.

The Psychology of It All

According to Frederick Herzberg, job security cannot increase job satisfaction, but the lack of it leads to job dissatisfaction.[1] Employees living in peril of losing their jobs are dissatisfied, and dissatisfied employees lack the motivation to perform well.

➲ Solutions

Employers, of course, cannot guarantee job security. Indeed, *their* jobs are also tenuous. But they can manage job insecurity by:

- Communicating honestly
- Helping employees to manage their long-term career
- Developing different methods to gain the commitment and loyalty of employees

Here are a few specific suggestions:

1. Promote ideals and values rather than company goals.
Management can gain a strong level of commitment and motivation by promoting socially desirable (rather than corporate) goals.

Employees are motivated by larger objectives, such as making the world a better place and improving the health of the community.

2. Don't deny the reality of the situation.
Employers must try not to cover up the fact that layoffs and re-structuring are part of today's economic reality. Telling employees they will have a job for life or that their jobs will be secure for many more years will only serve to decrease your credibility.

3. Help employees grow.
Creating an environment where training and skills improvement are encouraged will help any organization. True, the increased skills will help some employees find good jobs elsewhere. But it will also enable others to become more valuable contributors.

4. Provide portable benefits.
Rather than providing traditional pensions, employers should con-sider offering plans that allow employees to save for retirement with pre-tax dollars such as 401(k) and 403(b) plans. This way em-ployees can take the invested funds with them when they leave the firm. Employers should match contributions and provide them with retirement planning materials so they can make intelligent investment choices.

Conclusion

Job insecurity is here to stay, but employers can take proactive mea-sures to make it easier for employees to cope with this environment. Promoting organizational values, being honest with your employees, and providing long-term career assistance and portable benefits can all help.

Note

1. F. Herzberg et al. *Job Attitudes: Review of Research and Opinion* (Pittsburgh: Psychological Service of Pittsburgh, 1957).

❷❽

I've got no time for myself or my family.

I once consulted to a fast-paced, highly profitable retail firm that outsourced the manufacturing of its clothing to Hong Kong, Taiwan, Sri Lanka, and other distant locales with low labor costs. The hardworking, predominately female staff was sophisticated, competitive, and upwardly mobile. They worked hard, vying for promotions and pay increases. They operated in a high-pressure environment with frequently changing deadlines, constant worry about costs, and daily pushback from both clients and manufacturers.

The staff experienced a great deal of stress trying to balance work and family responsibilities. Many were required to travel often to Asia and maintain long hours. When they weren't traveling, the time difference between their East Coast office and the Asian manufacturers often required them to make late-hour telephone appointments from their homes. Many of the women had young families or were thinking about starting a family.

Most of the employees complained about their lack of life balance only to each other. Few wanted to jeopardize their promotion possibilities by tarnishing the personal credibility they had worked so hard to achieve. They were keenly aware that senior management was working the same long hours and not complaining about it.

The employee survey I conducted revealed their collective unhappiness to senior management. Their challenge was how to respond to these employee concerns without sacrificing the company's extremely high level of productivity.

The Problem for Employers

Poor work–life balance poses a dilemma for both employees and their employers. For employees, solutions such as working fewer hours or taking a less demanding job usually require major sacrifices, including less money, less meaningful work, and limited advancement opportunities.

For employers, providing employees with more time off and a slower work pace can adversely affect the bottom line. Venture capitalists, stockholders, and customers have little tolerance for the reduced speed and quality that may result from a more relaxed work environment.

Here are some reasons why employees have become dissatisfied with the balance between their work and personal lives:

1.   *Long Work Hours.* A survey commissioned by Expedia.com in 2006 revealed that more than a third of employed U.S. adults (38 percent) report regularly working more than 40 hours per week.[1]

2.   *Changing Demographics.* According to the Employment Policy Foundation's Center for Work and Family Balance, 66 percent of working households consisted of single-earner married couples in 1940. In 2006 it was 25 percent, and by 2030 it is expected to drop to 17 percent.[2] That means that in most households today there is no one home during the workday to run errands, take care of the children, or conduct routine tasks.

3.   *More Time in the Car.* Suburban sprawl has resulted in longer commuting times. It has also meant that children can no longer walk home from school or to their after-school activities. They need to be carpooled.

4. *Deterioration of Boundaries Between Work and Home.* Voice mail, e-mail, cell phones, laptops, and palm pilots have meant that the office is omnipresent. We just can't get away.

5. *Increased Work Pressure.* Job security is now an oxymoron. Employees feel that they must work longer hours to impress their bosses and keep their jobs.

6. *Inadequate Employer Responses.* Many progressive employers have actually made the problem worse by providing after-hour meals and such services as dry-cleaning and oil changes. Although well intentioned, these efforts have only made it easier for employees to work longer hours.

The Psychology of It All

Many employees are dissatisfied with their work–life balance because they do not feel in control of their work hours. As I mentioned earlier, these employees have a low "perception of control." They do not feel that they have the power to freely make decisions about when they will or won't work. This increases the stressfulness of their job.

In a report published by the Sloan Work and Family Research Network of Boston College, psychologists Allyson McElwain and Karen Korabik of the University of Guelph summarized the research literature on work family balance.[3] They state that:

- Work-family conflict occurs due to a specific type of stress in which two sets of pressures occur simultaneously, making it difficult to comply with both.

- For some, work interferes with family, and for others family interferes with work.

- Many employees experience guilt (i.e., feelings of remorse and responsibility) because they feel they are acting inconsistently with their own internal standards.

➲ Solutions

Employees define *work–life balance* in many different ways. For some, working 80 hours per week provides them with the balance they want. For others, working 40 hours disrupts their personal life. Employees often self-select themselves into particular professions and organizations based on the type of balance they want to achieve.

In the context of understanding these differences, there are a number of ways organizations can help employees achieve a more comfortable work–life balance:

1. Provide flexibility.

Many organizations devote substantial space in their employee handbooks in an attempt to carefully define such practices as work hours, time-off policies, and penalties for lateness. This only exacerbates the work–life balance. Employees and their supervisors become like Philadelphia lawyers, constantly seeking to bend the rules to accommodate what they both believe is the right thing to do.

Organizations should strive to create a work environment that provides employees with the day-to-day flexibility they need to manage the rest of their lives. The unwritten work rules become at least as important as written ones. For example, employees who typically work long hours and weekends should be given the freedom to come in late, leave early, or take time off during the middle of the day.

There are many different types of flexible work arrangements. Traditional flextime, for example, allows employees to vary their start- and end-times each day. A compressed work week enables employees to work more than eight hours per day, allowing them to work fewer days per week. And daily flextime allows them to work a different schedule each day. The Families and Work Institute of Boston College reports that employees who have access to flexible work arrangements are significantly more satisfied with their lives and experience less conflict between their jobs and their family lives than employees who don't have such arrangements.[4]

Providing employees with daily flextime enables them to maximize the control they have over their time and space. It not only reduces their general anxiety but provides them with the opportunity to achieve better balance by giving them time to attend special family events, visit a doctor during the day, or even go home to take a nap.

2. Educate supervisors.

First-line supervisors end up being the real makers and enforcers of time-off policies. Rather than following the written policies, they should be taught how to use compassion and common sense when making these types of decisions.

3. Become known as an organization where balance is valued.

In the past year I have worked with several organizations that make it known to employees and prospective employees that work–life balance is a key organizational value. They provide excellent benefits and work flexibility. At 5:00 P.M., employees are permitted—in fact, encouraged—to leave work. These organizations may not pay the highest salaries in the market, but their employees are highly committed and are willing to make sacrifices in their paychecks for a better lifestyle.

4. Reduce organizational inefficiencies.

Our research shows that more than half of employees feel the work in their departments is conducted inefficiently. Organizational inefficiency causes employees to work unnecessarily long hours. Involve employees in identifying and implementing solutions.

5. Provide senior management role models.
Employees often take their cues from the senior-most members of the organization. If they are workaholics, the rest of the organization will become workaholic. If they work hard to achieve balance in their lives, the rest of the organization will follow suit.

Conclusion

Management should set an example and use common sense rather than strict rules to create an environment that allows employees to create a balance between work and their personal lives. Not only is this possible, but it is often good for business.

Notes

1. "Expedia.com Survey Reveals Vacation Deprivation Among American Workers Is at an All-Time High," PRNewswire-FirstCall, May 23, 2006: http://biz.yahoo.com/prnews/060523/sftu098.html? .v = 56.

2. Rebecca Clay, "Making Working Families Work," APA Online, Volume 36, No. 11: http://www.apa.org/monitor/dec05/work .html.

3. A. K. McElwain and K. Korabik, "Work-Family Guilt." A Sloan Work and Family Encyclopedia entry: http://wfnetwork.bc.edu/ encyclopedia_entry.php?id = 270&area = All.

4. J. Casey, "Effective Workplace Series," *Work-Family Information on Flexible Work Schedules,* Issue 2, 2006.

29

Thirty-eight percent of employees do not feel their work provides them with a strong feeling of personal accomplishment.

I feel trapped. I wish I could go out on my own.

Back in 1993, when my boss at a major international consulting firm said, "Bruce, we are going to have to lay you off," I had mixed feelings. On the one hand, I was nervous about the future and about providing for my family. On the other hand, I felt a strong sense of relief. I would no longer have to worry about billable hours, impressing the bosses, and coping with internal politics.

But I also felt a strong sense of personal empowerment. For me, losing my job was like the scene from *Gone With the Wind* when Scarlett O'Hara returns at the end of the Civil War to Tara, the beautiful southern plantation where she had been raised. The Confederate Army had used the mansion as a military headquarters. All of the furniture, artwork, and of course, the slaves were gone. Her father had gone mad, and was walking around aimlessly. She was totally distraught. There was no food in the house and she was hungry. She went out to the fields, which had already been completely picked over, reached into the ground, grabbed a root, took a bite out of it, and shouted to the sky, "As God is my witness, as God is my witness they're not going to lick me. I'm going to live through this and when it's all over, I'll never be hungry again. No, nor any of my folk. If I have to lie, steal, cheat or kill. As God is my witness, I'll never be hungry again."

That's how *I* felt. I was determined to figure out a way to start my own consulting business so that I could support my family, never have to worry about being laid off again, be in charge of my own fate, sink or swim based on my own skills, and relish personally in my accomplishments rather than where I lay on management's scorecard.

Many years later, I feel a sense of personal accomplishment every day. When the phone rings, that's not an organization's phone I'm answering. It's *my* phone and *I* made it ring. Apparently I am not alone. According to the U.S. Census Bureau, in 2004 there were an estimated 10.4 million workers who had elected self-employment rather than working for an organization.[1]

The Problem for Employers

Many employees look back on their many years of service to their organization and say, "I don't really have anything to show for it." They lack a strong sense of personal accomplishment. They feel trapped in their job, but don't want a different one. What they really want to do is abandon the shackles of organizational life and go out on their own. They fantasize about starting their own business or consulting firm, but they're scared. They are terrified of taking the risk of leaving the security of their job. Many rationalize that they will make the leap once their kids are out of college, their mortgage is paid off, or they have saved enough money. They spend their idle time merely dreaming about what could have been.

This strong desire that many employees have to strike out on their own is a problem for their organizations. These employees possess valuable untapped energy, but instead of providing the organization with creativity and enthusiasm, they become a drain on the energy of others.

The Psychology of It All

Julian Rotter's social learning theory offers one explanation why people feel trapped in their jobs. His theory suggests that individuals differ in how much of an effect they believe they have on their environment.[2] His central concept is the continuum, "locus of control." Those with personalities more toward the external end of this continuum believe that what happens in their life is due to chance: events that are outside of their direct control. Taken to the extreme, these individuals are fatalists. At the other end of this continuum are internals. They believe that their fate is due largely to their own skills, abilities, and the actions they take.

On the one hand, individuals who have a more external "locus of control" feel powerless to leave their jobs. They lack the belief that they really *can* have a major impact on their own destiny. If they do fantasize about starting their own business, they think the only way that would happen is through a fortuitous series of events. On the other hand, those with an internal "locus of control" are inclined to believe that they can take risks in their life and that they will be able to take control of their future. They are the ones who are more likely to leave to work for themselves.

"Objectivism" provides another explanation of why people feel trapped in their jobs. Ayn Rand, the founder of this school of thought, argued that the reason people succeed or fail in life is due to whether or not they "choose to think." She writes, "A man can choose to think or to let his mind stagnate, or he can choose actively to turn against his intelligence, to evade his knowledge, to subvert his reason. If he refuses to think, he courts disaster."[3]

Extrapolating this principle to the workplace, employees who feel trapped at their jobs and too paralyzed to venture out on their own may not be choosing to think. They may be failing to use their minds to control their reality.

➲ Solutions

Here are several ways that organizations can harness the entrepreneurial spirit of employees and provide them with a strong sense of accomplishment:

1. Begin an intrapreneurship program.

Some organizations establish intrapreneurship programs to provide promising employees with the financial and emotional support they need to launch a new business within the organization. For example, let's say an enthusiastic chemist in a pharmaceutical lab discovers a promising new compound, but the compound is unrelated to the type of drugs the company currently produces. Instead of risking the employee leaving for another job or to start his own business, the company can fund that new business. Or a medical claims specialist working in a small practice might say, "I can bring in more money by providing my services to other medical practices." If the idea makes sense, the practice could fund a new business venture to become the outsourcer for other organizations.

This can be a win-win situation for the employee and the organization. The company keeps the employee from leaving and stands to gain a great deal financially if the new business is successful. The employee stands to profit financially, while gaining a strong sense of personal accomplishment.

2. Allow employees to work part-time.

Instead of losing employees when they want to start their own business in a different field, offer them the opportunity to work part-time. This will provide them with a safety net and the organization may not lose much because many employees can actually produce the same amount of work on a part-time basis as they can working full time.

Conclusion

Employees itching to go out on their own will resent management for preventing them from fulfilling their dreams. Organizations should consider helping them start a new profit center within the company or offering them part-time employment.

Notes

1. U.S. Bureau of Labor Statistics, "Self-Employed Workers by Industry and Occupation," *Employment Earnings Monthly,* January issue, Table 593: http://www.bls.gov/cps/home.htm.

2. J. B. Rotter, "Generalized Expectancies for Internal vs. External Control of Reinforcement," *Psychological Monographs* 80, 609 (1966).

3. Ayn Rand, *Atlas Shrugged* (New York: Penguin Group, 1957).

❸⓿

Thirty-eight percent of employees don't feel committed to their organization.

My company isn't committed to me, so why should I be committed to it?

I have a friend who owns a small, second-generation family-owned auto parts distributorship. He employs about thirty people. His employees receive orders from customers, order parts from suppliers, make deliveries, and keep the books. It's not glamorous work and doesn't provide the same level of pay or benefits that some of his workers might earn if they were able to land a job with a larger company.

You would think that employee turnover would be high, but it's not. My friend rarely loses employees. The average tenure is more than fifteen years. Why?

Carrying on the tradition of his father, he deals with his employees fairly and maintains his loyalty to them. He provides health insurance and a 401(k) plan. If an employee has a personal or financial problem, he helps him out. If the company has an off year, nobody loses their job. If business is slow, he takes home less pay himself and makes certain his workers receive their checks on time. He treats them with respect and gets to know them as people, not just as employees.

But this is not what it's like in most organizations, where employees are typically disloyal and their organizations are disloyal to them. That's become the way of the world. You hear about it every day: large companies laying off tens of thousands of workers, cutting medical benefits, and eliminating bankrupt retirement plans.

We have become accustomed to believing that:

- Loyalty is an outmoded idea, no longer relevant.
- The only thing that really matters in the work world is money.
- Maintaining loyalty to your employer is a foolish career strategy.
- Maintaining loyalty to your employees is impractical in today's economy.

The Problem for Employers

Employee turnover is extremely expensive for organizations, often amounting to 150 percent or more of an employee's annual salary. The financial costs include lost productivity while positions are left vacant, as well as the costs of recruiting, hiring, and training new employees. There are also more subtle costs, including reduced commitment from employees who were friends of the person who left, and loss of teamwork and camaraderie now that the team has been disrupted.

The Psychology of It All

Recall that equity theory asserts that individuals try to maintain a balance between what they contribute to their work (e.g., skills, knowledge, effort, and commitment to their employer) and what they get out of their work (e.g., compensation and loyalty). When this balance is disrupted, people will often try to correct the situation by reducing their inputs. Equity theory predicts that when people feel that their employer is not committed to them, they will reduce their feelings of inequity by decreasing their commitment to the organization.

➲ Solutions

Call me old-fashioned, but are the following thoughts mere relics of the past, or can they still have validity in today's harsh world?

- If I am loyal to my company, my company will be loyal to me.

- I want my company to be an extension of who I am, just like my family.

- I want to look back on my career and feel good about the many years I devoted to this company.

- I value the people I work with.

- I really believe in what this organization stands for and will stick with it through thick and thin.

Likewise, can the following thoughts employers used to have about maintaining loyalty to their employees still be relevant today?

- If we are loyal to our employees, they will be loyal to us.

- We want to be one big happy family here where everyone is focused on the same goal.

- We value long service and will reward those who stay with us.

- We will provide good retirement benefits for those who maintain their loyalty to us.

- Employees are our most valuable assets.

- We have invested much in our employees. They possess valuable knowledge about our history, our customers, and our products and services. We need to keep them with us to capitalize on our investment.

If these views still resonate with you and your organization, here is what you can do:

1. Fight rather than succumb to the prevailing trend.
Become a maverick in your industry. Make it known that contrary to other employers, you do value loyalty from your employees and

will reciprocate. Offer a pension. Offer generous benefits. Even consider offering long-term employment contracts. Dare to be different because you know it's the right thing to do and in fact will have a positive effect on your business.

2. Rethink the economics.

You may be wondering how you can possibly afford to do this. It may not seem practical, but it is possible.

- The cost of employee turnover is very high. Finding replacements and training new hires is expensive.

- Operating a company where employees are constantly looking to bolt lowers employee morale and productivity.

- Your employees might be willing to receive less pay if they value the benefits, pension, and other guarantees. This is not uncommon. Just ask those who work in many government and public education jobs.

3. Make loyalty to employees a core value in your organization.

Rarely do you see "Loyalty to Employees" in an organization's list of corporate values. If you believe it is important, it should be there. All strategic decisions of the company should be made with this core value in mind.

4. Be willing to make sacrifices to maintain employee loyalty.

In order to maintain employee loyalty you may need to make sacrifices, such as:

- Slowing down corporate growth to a more controlled level
- Placing limits on annual pay increases
- Insourcing rather than outsourcing work
- Investing in retraining of employees

Conclusion

Loyalty to employees has become a forgotten relic in much of the work world. It doesn't have to be that way. In fact, making loyalty a corporate value can actually improve your long-term bottom line.

Summary: What You Can Do

So, what can you do if the employees in your organization are unhappy and hate you? In some organizations, of course, management doesn't care. They view employees as expendable and nonessential. Many others do nothing about unhappy employees because they feel powerless to solve the problem. They are under the mistaken assumption that all employees really want is more money. Since they are unwilling or unable to pay more, they simply ignore the cries of their employees.

But I can cite many examples of organizations that have successfully reduced the unhappiness of employees in their organizations. They have proven that addressing employee concerns can and does work. Here are several suggestions for what *you* can do in your own organization:

1. *Listen to employees.* Identify the real problems by conducting focus groups or an employee survey. Using an outside objective facilitator or survey organization can help assuage employee concerns about their anonymity. Organizations committed to reducing employee unhappiness listen to their employees on a regular basis.

2. *Involve employees in developing solutions.* Organizations that are most successful in addressing the concerns of employees involve them in action planning. Employees can develop solutions to problems that would never occur to management.

3. *Start small, and big things will happen.* I have worked in many organizations with unhappy employees where management did not know how to begin to solve the problems. They decided to focus on

just one or two areas. For example, an electronic equipment manufacturer decided to make certain their performance reviews were conducted on time. An insurance company adopted flextime. A retailer
instituted quarterly briefings from the president to all employees. In
all of these cases, addressing just one important concern had a dra-
matic positive effect on employee morale. It stopped the crying, not
only on this one issue, but also on many issues.

*   *   *

Reducing employee unhappiness is not only good for business;
it's good for all of us. Employees spend the majority of their waking
hours at their jobs. Doesn't it make sense to provide them with a work
environment where they can feel supported, respected, and fulfilled?

Epilogue: A Lesson from the Future

The second *Star Trek* movie, *The Wrath of Khan* (my favorite) opens on the bridge of the starship Enterprise in the twenty-third century, with Saavik, played by a very svelte Kirstie Alley, sitting in the Captain's chair. We can see from her long pointy ears that she's a Vulcan.

The communications officer, Uhura, reports to her that there is a distress signal coming from a fuel-carrying vessel called the Kobuyashi Maru. The problem is that the vessel is in the "neutral zone," an area that Federation vessels cannot enter according to treaty.

Saavik makes the command decision to enter the neutral zone to rescue the crew of the Kobuyashi Maru. She orders Lieutenant Commander Sulu to chart a course for the vessel and asks that the transporter room get ready to beam the survivors aboard. As they enter the neutral zone, Spock announces from his station, "We are now in violation of treaty."

The computer informs the crew on the bridge that three enemy Klingon cruisers are headed toward them. Communications Officer Uhura attempts to notify the Klingons that they are merely on a rescue mission. The Klingons do not respond and begin to power up their weapons.

Saavik orders the crew to take their battle stations and raise the shields. A battle ensues. When the Klingons fire their phasers, Saavik orders evasive maneuvers and the return of fire. She eventually also orders the release of the powerful photon torpedoes.

Saavik keeps her cool as the computer calmly reports, "Shields are down to 75 percent . . . shields are down to 40 percent." Most of the crew on the bridge, including Spock, are killed during the battle. The shields continue to lose strength. The computer voice then says, "Warning, shields are down to 5 percent," and the movie goes totally dark.

Now, of course, you know the movie isn't over. It has just started. The lights on the bridge come back on and we see that everyone is okay. We learn that Saavik is a cadet in Starfleet Academy and that the Kobuyashi Maru is a training simulation, a no-win scenario meant to test the skills of a cadet. No matter what orders she would have given, they all would have died.

We learn, however, that there is one person in the entire history of Star Fleet Academy who has been able to pass the Kobuyashi Maru simulation. If you haven't guessed already, yes, it's Captain James T. Kirk, now an admiral.

For the entire movie, as they are fighting Khan, played by Ricardo Montalban, Saavik keeps asking Kirk how he was able to succeed with the simulation. She tells him that she has been through it billions of times in her mind (Vulcans can do this you know) and could not understand how he did it. Near the end of the movie he finally tells her: "The night before the test I went into the control room and reprogrammed the simulation so that it was possible to rescue the ship."

*　*　*

The moral of this story is not that you should cheat on exams, but that you have to do things differently. If you keep managing your employees in the same way, you are going to achieve the same results. Employees are going to continue to be resentful and hate you. Starting today, make up your mind that you are going to do things differently.

Recommended Readings

S elected sources that highlight the effect that roles, group dynamics, and intergroup relations have on the behavior of individuals in organizations:

Janis, I. L. *Victims of Groupthink: A Psychological Study of Foreign-Policy Decisions and Fiascos.* Boston, Mass.: Houghton Mifflin Company, 1972.

Smith, K. K. *Groups in Conflict: Prisons in Disguise.* Dubuque, Iowa: Kendall/Hunt Publishing Company, 1982.

Zimbardo, P. G., and G. White. Stanford Prison Experiment Slide-Tape Show (Stanford University, 1972): prisonexp.org.

Selected books on managing and motivating employees:

Branham, L. *The 7 Hidden Reasons Employees Leave.* New York: AMA-COM, 2005.

Buckingham, M., and C. Coffman. *First Break All the Rules: What the World's Greatest Managers Do Differently.* New York: Simon & Schuster, 1999.

Campbell, M. J. *Five Gifts of Insightful Leaders.* Newton, Mass.: Charlesbank Press, 2006.

Carroll, S. J., Jr. *Performance Appraisal and Review Systems: The Identification, Measurement, and Development of Performance in Organizations.* Glenview, Ill: Scott, Foresman and Company, 1982.

Collins, J. *Good to Great: Why Some Companies Make the Leap . . . and Others Don't.* New York: HarperCollins, 2001.

Fournies, F. *Why Employees Don't Do What They're Supposed to Do and What to Do About It.* New York: McGraw-Hill, 1999.

Hackman, J. R., E. E. Lawler III, and L. W. Porter. *Perspectives on Behavior in Organizations.* New York: McGraw-Hill Book Company, 1977.

Herzberg, F. W. *Work and the Nature of Man.* New York: The World Publishing Company, 1973.

Lawler, E. E. III. *Motivation in Organizations.* Monterey, Calif.: Brooks/Cole Publishing Company, 1973.

Miner, J. B. The *Challenge of Managing.* Philadelphia: W. B. Saunders Company, 1975.

Nash, A. N., and S. J. Carroll, Jr. *The Management of Compensation.* Monterey, Calif.: Brooks/Cole Publishing Company, 1975.

Porter, L. W., E. E. Lawler III, and J. R. Hackman. *Behavior in Organizations.* New York: McGraw-Hill Book Company, 1975.

Schein, E. H. *Organizational Culture and Leadership.* San Francisco: Jossey-Bass, Inc. Publishers, 1985.

Sirota, D., L. Mischkind, and M. Meltzer. *The Enthusiastic Employee: How Companies Profit by Giving Workers What They Want.* Philadelphia: Wharton School of Publishing, 2005.

Steers, R. M., and L. W. Porter. *Motivation and Work Behavior.* New York: McGraw-Hill Book Company, 1975.

Taylor, F. *The Principles of Scientific Management.* New York: W.W. Norton & Company, Inc., 1967.

Wanous, J. P. *Organizational Entry: Recruitment, Selection, and Socialization of Newcomers.* Reading, Mass.: Addison-Wesley Publishing Company, 1980.

Books on consulting, self-employment, and building a business:

Gerber, M. E. *The E-Myth Revisited: Why Most Small Businesses Don't Work and What to Do About It.* New York: HarperCollins Publishers, Inc., 1995.

Katcher, B. L. *The Consultant's Corner: Practical Advice and Insights for*

Beginning and Experienced Consultants. 2006, e-book downloadable at http://www.discoverysurveys.com/store.html.

Weiss, A. *Million Dollar Consulting: The Professionals Guide to Growing a Practice.* New York: McGraw-Hill, Inc., 1992.

Index

About the Authors

Bruce L. Katcher, Ph.D., is an industrial/organizational psychologist and founder of Discovery Surveys, Inc., a management-consulting firm based outside Boston in Sharon, Massachusetts. Since 1993, he has been helping organizations better understand and delight their employees and customers. His firm conducts employee opinion surveys and customer satisfaction surveys.

Bruce delivers keynote addresses on *Why Employees Hate Their Managers and What You Can Do About It, How to Address the Major Complaints of Employees, How to Improve Your Listening Skills, The 21 Secrets of Finding a Job, How to Jump Start Your Consulting Business,* and *How to Really Enjoy What You Eat.*

Clients for whom he has conducted surveys include: Alcoa Mill Products, BBN Technologies, Delta Dental Plan, Invensys, Johnson & Johnson, Manulife Financial, the Massachusetts Medical Society, Mayo Clinic, Science Magazine, Revlon, Sodexho USA, Textron Systems, Timberland, Worcester Polytechnic Institute, and W.R. Grace.

For more information, visit www.DiscoverySurveys.com.

* * *

Adam Snyder has for thirty years been helping individuals and organizations communicate their messages to employees, customers, and the public. He has coauthored books with top business leaders, and his byline can be found in dozens of publications. He is also president of the animation company, Rembrandt Films LLC, a producer and distributor of classic cartoons from around the world.